# CONTENTS

# ABOUT ME

Interview with Dean Holness

I started out playing football as soon as I could walk, I then went on to play for my school, district and county teams. Eventually joining the youth team for Bromley Town FC at 16, before moving to play in the 1st team of semi-professional out fit Dulwich Hamlet, where I was voted as the non-league player to watch for the future in 1995.

I then went on trial with Crystal Palace. I was offered a professional contract at the age of 19, but when the contract fell through at the last minute, I left the country to play for professional football team Umea FC in Sweden.

When I came back to England I took a few years out from football to start acting in Sky 1 tv drama 'Dreamteam' and feature film 'Mike Bassett England Manager'.

Before coming back to football and signing a short term professional football contract with Southend Untied FC at the age of 25.

I enjoyed playing football, travelling to different countries, playing with and against some great players.

But it hasn't always been easy and that's what lead me to write this book, to offer help and guidance to others looking to become professional footballers.

I'm also an FA intermediary which will allow me to help and guide players through their careers, setting up their futures and getting the best for them.

For more info contact: info@deanholness.co.uk

www.deanholness.co.uk

2

# FOOTBALL

3

Football is a global sport loved by billions of people all over the world, you could say that its the world's biggest sporting pastime played and watched in every continent, with young and old sharing the dream of scoring that all important match winning goal. From children growing up wanting to be professionals travelling the world, watched and loved by millions, touched by their genius and artistry. To the devoted fans enjoying some of their best moments in life watching from the sidelines or on television. Football is in our hearts, and if we are lucky enough to be graced with the talent, desire and dedication to play at the highest levels, then we should grab that opportunity with both hands.

The professional football game has many different routes into it. From a young boy rising up through the ranks and making their debut in front of a packed sell out crowd, or playing semi professionally before getting scouted and bought by a club, to being spotted by a scout and asked to come along to train with an academy/professional teams reserves side or even better being asked to train with the first team. All of this can happen at any time in your young life and when it does you'll want to be as ready as you possibly can.

For some being a professional is all they have ever dreamed of, from collecting the football stickers and trading them in the school playground to watching their favourite team playing on television. Spending everyday with a football playing anywhere they can, kicking it against the wall in the playground or park. Whether it's for fun with their friends in a 1v1/2v2 game or full on competitive 11 a-side match.. Constantly trying to develop the skills and techniques used by their favourite players just as I did when I was younger. But most of all just enjoying playing the beautiful game.

This book is for both players and parents, to help you get the most out of your talent and maximise your chances of making a career out of the thing you love, football.

## IS IT FOR YOU?

Professional football isn't for everybody. It takes a lot of aspects (mind, body, life and chance) to go right at the right time, some of these things you're in control of, but others you're not. Even the most talented footbballers might not make it professionally where as others who are not so talented will.

Unfortunately the fact is that a huge number of young kids won't make it into the professional game, and if they do even fewer of them will get to play for a top club or their country. It is suggested that the ratio of players that make it into the professional game is 1% from youth academy/development centres around the country. There are many reasons for this, some are just not good enough to play at a professional level and playing at a semi professional level is the highest they will achieve (which is still an achievement in itself). Some will have suffered bad injuries before even getting the chance to prove themselves making them unable to compete at a professional level and some will fall out of love with playing the game at such a high competitive level because of all the other aspects that go with playing football at that high level.

But for those lucky few the world is your oyster.

## MODERN DAY FOOTBALL

The modern game of football is forever changing on and off the field. On the field the players have to be more then just footballers, they have to be athletes with a very high physical and  flexible level of fitness. They have to be able to run faster, longer and be strong for great lengths of time. They have to play lots of games per season and enter as many tournaments as possible, with more tournaments being played then ever before.

The modern day top footballer is now a global superstar, as big as some pop and movie stars, with more influence on people that watch football then before. This can be a great world to inhabit not to mention a very lucrative and luxurious

# DREAM COMES TRUE

## Soccer soap star is so talented Southend have signed him...

WING WIZARD – Dean Holness, who stars out wide as Campbell Hooper for Harchester in the hit Sky One show Dream Team (left), has been signed up in real life to play on the wing for Southe

**KEAT EXCLUSIVE**

one to. But it's very easy to see how a young person can lose their head and way in all of this, usually because they're being ill advised or not being advised at all. Again this all depends on what level of football you are playing, as the level increases so does the pressure, money and fame making the very top often hard to manage and often a cutthroat business.

The way the game has changed so significantly is partly due to extremely wealthy millionaire and billionaire owners taking over clubs, making them their new play-things. With huge amounts of money being invested into clubs the new owners want the best and will stop at nothing to get it. Television companies such as Sky and BT Sports showing more games then ever before with dedicated channels showing all the big games this gives football teams even more money to spend each year on buying players and paying their players higher and higher wages. Global and iconic brands such as Nike, Adidas, Puma and Under Armor pumping huge amounts of money into football teams just to be their kit makers and spon-sors so they can get their companies name on the front of the team's shirts. Amaz-ing advertisements shown all around the world to billions of people.

To some a footballers life couldn't be sweeter, but the reality is that this is not all footballers. To give you an idea, the number of players that are involved in English football are 92 teams split over four major professional leagues. If we say that each team has at least 32 players (11 first team & 5 subs, 11 reserves & 5 subs) that's 32 x 92 = 2,944 players playing football in England and well under 100 of them will become mega stars and sign major contracts, sponsorship and advertising deals. leaving the rest to work hard on saving their money for once their career is over.


## HOW TO GET AHEAD

However high you want to aim whether it's semi-professional or professional it's good to be realistic about your opportunities. Here are some ideas of how best to set your goals and realise your ambitions.

1.Set yourselves short-term realistic goals:
If you stick to this it will have a long-term effect. By doing this you will accomplish much more, because success will breed success. Achievement and success are feelings that we all love, driving us to get that feeling again and again. As an example, if you're a striker and you say to yourself "I'm going to score 20 more goals then any other striker this season" or you are a defender and you say "no one will score against us in the next 15 games" the odds of reaching those goals are not balanced in your favour. By putting yourself under this pressure and then ultimately not reaching these targets you will make yourself feel like a failure, when actually you're not.

This will ultimately affect your game making you try too hard and make wrong decisions in matches. With the knock on effect of bringing your confidence down and leaving you fighting a battle with yourself and your opponent. (not a good place to be in). But if you say "I will aim to score in every 5-6 games" or "I will not let anyone score in the next 10 minutes" then you have a higher chance of reaching those targets and once you have achieved these targets then you will set yourself another one improving each and every time. Slowly but surely you will reach a very high and consistent level of playing which is where you want to be.

2. Keep it realistic and achievable:
Remember everyone's levels will be different; some will be greater than others. So assess yourself as accurately as you can, look at your achievements over a period of time, maybe a month or even half a season and start working towards your personal goals.
Forwards targets should go like this, score every 6-5 games, then 5-4 games, then 4-3 games, and 3-2 games.

Defenders (including keepers) should look like this no goals within 5-10 minutes, 10-15 minutes, then 15-20 minutes, then 25-30 minutes, then 30-35 minutes until you can make a whole half.

8

Wingers and Midfielders aim to score: 5-10 goals, then 10-15 goals, then 15-20 goals a season in all competitions. And set-up 5-10 goals, 10-15 goals, 15-20 goals, 20-25 goals a season in all competitions. Start with the lowest and work your way up until you find YOUR level and do you best not to drop underneath it.

## COPING WITH THE UPS AND DOWNS

This is something that most people find hard to understand, but something that you have to accept and accept fast is, you can't win them all. Losing is something that we are not accustomed to and don't like. Even as a child losing to your brother, sister or cousin at a game maybe made you feel as if they'd done something under-handed to win, and sometimes left you feeling like you'd been cheated.

Football is of course a highly competitive sport and when you play in tournaments you should always walk into an arena or playing field with passion, drive and a will to win every game. But the reality is that you can't win everything, sometimes you or your team will be out classed, out played, not at your best and second to everything. In these situations sometimes you know what you or your team need to do to improve however, at other times it will be harder to accept especially if you know that you have played better than your opponent, done more then enough to win the game. but despite all your efforts the result doesn't go your way.

You may have already played in competitive matches where you would have had the upper hand, around 80% of the ball and attacking game, having 20 shots on goal compared to their 1, but still come off the pitch drawing or even worse losing. At this point you may feel let down, cheated, saying "If the referee only got that one decision right," or "If the rest of the team pulled their weight," or "I did everything I could." But the truth is that no matter what you say the result will always stand and can't be reversed. The best approach to deal with something like this is to say something along the lines of "I'm absolutely gutted that we've lost, but it's all behind me now and whatever improvements need to be made, will be made before the next one."

We can all point the finger and shout at others, as that's the easy way, and sometimes that's needed to get things out in the open or to clear the air. But what is harder to do is to look at ourselves and say "could I have done more," or "what didn't I do in this game that I will do in the next one" or "what did the other team do that we didn't?"

Now imagine that for every bad game or loss, a 5 pound weight was put around your neck which you will carry around until you can set it down to one side, whether its in a game or at training. So if you lose one game, then you have a bad training session and lose another game, then you'll have 15 pounds of weight hanging around you and your mind. Now you are finding it hard to move and concentrate, causing you to be unfocused and heavy headed, failing to reach your normal level of achievements. If you can move or set aside these set backs quickly, the less weight you"ll have hanging around you and your mind, allowing you to be focused and enthusiastic, giving you a better chance of winning more matches and getting you quickly back to the consistent high level of football you're capable of.

One thing about playing competitive football is that your games will come thick and fast, this will give you a chance to quickly rectify mistakes made within the same week and get back that confidence in yourself needed to play high quality football. But this pace of games can also destroy you just as quickly by digging yourself into a hole and digging deeper and deeper each week, making you lose confidence and finding yourself not wanting the ball.

You have to look at your game not over every touch or run you've made but over the game as a whole, try thinking of a footballer as a bit like a stock market trader.

They make many deals everyday, some deals are good and some deals are bad, but they don't look at each and every trade they've made because they will fluctuate so much, so they look at how the day has gone as a whole. At the end of every week or month they will look back at how many good days they've had compared to how many bad days and make sure that the good days outweigh the bad days. This is a healthy way to approach your football season, try looking at performances month to month or every 4-5 games and see how many good games you've had to bad games. Your aim will be to make your good games outweigh your bad ones by at least 3-1. But be mindful that you'll need to be very honest with yourself about how you've played, if you think it's somewhere in the middle then that can be classed as an average game which you will still want to turn into good games by the end of a few months. The higher and longer you can keep your level of playing the more you will enjoy your football and the harder it will be for the manager to keep you out of the team.

## A LITTLE SOMETHING EXTRA

A huge part of life and football is about relationships. Meeting new people that you have to get along with trust and have faith in, is something that we're constantly learning to manage. Right from the start and all the way through your career the world of football can seem like a lonely place. Sometimes you may get the feeling that you don't fit in or belong and that people are talking about you, or that a few of your team members dislike you or are jealous of you. If you learn how to deal with these issues at a young age the easier it will be to cope with when you get older. Knowing how to handle people, their ways and comments is a unique skill in itself, people will always want to tell you how good or bad you are and what's best for you. Learn to know yourself what your worth, believe in your abilities, because if you don't believe in yourself then it will be hard for others to believe in you. Teach this to yourself and your children. Whatever advice or criticism they may encounter to take it on board, process it and then reach their own outcome.

11

Don't let what's been said knock your confidence or faith in yourself, learn from it and believe in your abilities.

Enjoy yourself in all that you do, whether it's on or off the field. Your footballing career won't last that long, in fact the average top flight professional footballing career in England is around 9 -10 years, as is the case with most physical sports. But compare that to the average life expectancy in the UK of 79.5 years and you'll see that playing professional football will make up a very small percentage of your life. If you've been fortunate enough to have made a career doing something that you enjoy and love then you'll want to look back at it having given it your all, with happiness and no regrets.

*"To keep grafting,listening and taking on board advice. Be humble and have bags of humility. Respect and talk to absolutely everyone as the fall from grace can be very sharp"*

## Danny Mills: Charlton Athletic & Brighton

*"Work as hard as you can, be the best you can be. When you don't give your all, that's failing, when you give your all that's winning"*

## Leon McKenzie: Crystal Palace, Norwich & Coventry City

*"Dedication put down your computer practice, if it doesn't work out at one club go to another, football doesn't owe you anything"*

## Chris kamara: Swindon Town, Brentford & Stoke City

*"Enjoy it because being a professional footballer is a really short career, be wise with your money and think ahead.. Unless your a top player earning top money then you will need a new career later in life"*

## Charlie Macdonald: Brentford, Milton Keynes Dons & Oldham Athletic

# YOUTH YEARS

# FINDING A LOCAL CLUB/PLAYING FOR A TEAM

So your son/daughter is around 4-5 years old and has been playing football in the house, garden and just about anywhere they can. But now they want to get into playing with others, maybe for a team but you don't know where to start.

Most local areas run fun football weekend schemes that let under 6s play and learn the basics of football: kicking a ball, running around cones, co-ordinating skills and learning to take direction. Most competitive football teams don't start picking boys/girls until they are 6 years old (under 7s), so you'll find that you may have to stick with playing in the park or with one of these weekend schemes until then. You can use the internet to help you find them. You can also look in the local newspapers at the sports section to see if there are any advertisements for players, or to see where these teams train and play so you can go along to a match and ask the manager directly if your child can join.

Once your son/daughter reaches the age where they can train and play with a team it's a good idea to speak to parents at your childs school to find out the names of local football teams in your area or if any of their friends are playing for a local club to see if your child can go along to training with them. At this age boys and girls can play on the same team, its only once they reach the age of 15/16 that they have to play for different teams, this will change in the near future.

Finding a team can be a very strange process as you may find that some parents aren't that helpful in telling you where to go as you may join their child's team and take their child's position in the team. Its better to start looking for teams at the beginning of a season which is usually around the end of June to the begining of August as teams have a allocated amount of players that can join the and be registered with the league before the season starts, during the season teams are general full unless players drop out. But if you ask enough friends and parents then you will eventually find a team. You may need to trial a few teams until you find the one that's right for you and your child, most important of all when looking for a team is that your child enjoys the training and likes the coach.

This will be a major factor in the progress of your childs football. You may find that your child may attend quite a few training sessions before they are actually picked to play a competitive match. However as long as your child is enjoying it, getting good training, and learning to develop the basic skills there will be plenty of time to play competitive football matches (plus at this age the football matches are alll non competitive until under 11s).

Something to bear in mind is that the majority of these teams are run by parents who take the time out of work to help, support and manage the club so things may not always go as smooth and professional as you'd like. This includes the training that your child may be getting there, so be patient with the manager and the other parents and players that are involved in the team. As a parent its great if you can help out in anyway you can. Your child will have to show that they can be a team player and have the willingness to listen and learn.

You will usually have to pay for your child to play for a football team or to attend one of these football weekend schools. This can vary in price from team to team so look around at different teams to find one that you can afford. You may have to pay a joining fee to help pay for your childs kit and where they train, it may be a weekly or monthly fee.

## STARTING TRAINING

The whole process of training maybe new to your child, learning the many different types of football exercises, drills, and the rules, will be harder for some children than for others. This may make you feel like your child is far behind or that they should think about taking up a different sport. Try not to get frustrated with your child as this could put them off playing football or any sport for that matter. Your child may even be feeling how you are, so you will need to be encouraging, supportive and patient. Talk to your child and ask them what they find hard and what they find easy as this could lead you both down the right path.

Something to bear in mind is that most young boys and girls learn things differently especially when it comes to physical activity. A key skill when learning to play football is processing information given to you and demonstrating that you've understood that information correctly.

Here are three ways in which people can learn:

1, Visually - being shown/seeing how to do something.
2, Speech - being told how to do something.
3, Practical - physically trying what you've been taught.

Most people usually have one style they respond better too. For example in school when the teacher is reading to the class or telling the class what to do, the children that take information in better visually find it harder to follow and become distracted, which can lead to getting the next part of that lesson wrong. If the same teacher showed these kids the same story with pictures or acted out the scenes the kids would find it more interesting and would follow and understand the lesson better. The same principles apply with football coaching; the children that learn visually will pay more attention and learn when the coach is showing them what to do but at the same time others who respond better to being told what to do instead of being shown, may get left behind.
Find out the way your child learns best and help them with the areas they are not so good at, by doing this you will be able to help them progress not only in football but in school as they would have developed a new way of learning allowing them to soak up more information.

While at this young age it is good practice for your child to play in as many different positions as possible. This will help them learn and understand all aspects of the game. Plus you, your child and the manager will be able to see the position/positions that best suits your child. Sometimes the best position isn't always the one your child likes to play in.

For example some children start out wanting to be Centre Forwards because of the joy they get from scoring goals, but actually they make better defenders then the defenders already in their own team. You may notice this when you put the fast Forward at Centre Back and no one can get past them, and if they do get passed the defender they are fast enough to get the ball back. Likewise if you put the big Centre Back up front and their to strong for the other team and have a powerful shot making them score lots of goals.

Expect that your child's football development will be a slow process but eventually it will click and will seem as if by magic they can play and understand the basics of football. Try not to be too hard on yourself or your child by trying to speed up this process, patience, excitement and enjoyment is all what's needed at this young age.

From the ages of 5-12 don't expect too much from your child or that they are going to be the next best thing even if they are really good, they are just starting out and have many lesson to learn. Believe it or not some professional and ex professional footballers didn't even start playing football until they were over the age of 12 and in their teens.

# OTHER PLACES TO PLAY/SCHOOL AND DISTRICT TEAMS

Most primary schools have a football team and will play against other local schools which is fun and maybe where your child will encounter their first match. This is great for them as they will be playing with lots of friends which can make it easier to participate. To get into the school team, playing football in the playground at break-time is a great start as the teachers all watch the children there. Some schools have a sign up sheet or after school team, however some afterschool teams you may have to pay for depending on your school. You can generally ask the school sports teacher how to get your child into the team. There may not be space for you at first or you may have to be in the older age group but be patient as people will drop out or you will eventually be old enough to join.

Playing for your district or county team is good thing for your child to get into, as the process of getting into the team will show them that its a lot of hard work (and its even harder to get into a professional team!). They will need to attend trials which can last up to 3-4 weeks, so as a parent be prepared to run your child around from one place to another which maybe early in the mornings or just as you finish work. Some district teams may only tell you that your child has been picked to play a match the day before which can be a pain to have to organise but something that you should be ready to deal with.

Getting into your district team is usually done this way. Either the district manager or scout will see your child playing for their local team, your child's school sports teacher may put them forward or alternatively be able to tell you when the next trial dates are and may have a contact for you. There may also be a contact on the internet if you search for district football teams in your local area, but don't forget to enter your child's age as there may not be a team for your child's age group.

After trials and friendly matches the manager will get his squad of players down to 15-17. This may be the first time that your child will have encountered going on trial and the first time that they may have faced being rejected if they didn't get picked. If this is the case be prepared that this may cause your child to say that they don't want to play football anymore because they feel they aren't good enough or don't like the rejection. At this point it will be hard to know what to do, you don't want to feel like your pressurising your child into playing but you also don't want them to quit at the first hurdle or the first sign of disappointed. Give them time let them play with friends and try to forget about the rejection. Take the time to explain to them that this will happen in football quite a bit and even top players have been releasd or dropped to the subs bench in their careers. However there will be other teams and other managers that will want you to play for them, so keep going and keep playing so these managers can see you play and pick you for their team.

When playing for the district or county you child will play against other district and county teams, these matches won't be every week like when they play for their Sunday league team but will be more like every 2-3 weeks or even once a month. They will also be playing against other players that have been through the same process to get into their team, so the level of football can be much higher then when they play for their Sunday team.

Professional scouts attend district and county matches because they know that the standard of football will be high and that these players have all had a trial to get into the team, which will be the how they will get into a professional teams academy or development centre.

You can play for your district, county and Sunday league team all at the same time, but this can be a bit too much for your young growing child. So monitor how many games and training sessions they are doing a week or month because they are

21

growing and can easily get growth problems which can effect them for rest of their lives. One such problem is Osgood- Schlatter disease, which is an activity related pain that occurs a few inches below the kneecap, or patella on the front of the knee. This happens commonly to children between the ages of 9-16 years both boys and girls who are equally vulnerable to it. Sports that require lots of running, jumping, kneeling, and squatting are particularly associated with this disease. It's impossible to stop your child from growing but you can help them from getting such growing pains by:

1, Not letting them play so many physical activities.
Limit there after school activities, remember when they aren't with you and at school everyday they will definitely be playing some sort of activity that involves running.
2, Relaxing and stretching the body and muscles giving them time to do what they need to do (grow).
3, Eating healthily as your child is growing and will now also be eating you out of house and home but you need to make sure they get the right food for them to eat which will support their growth, body and mind. Giving it all the nutrients that it needs.

There are some exercises, stretches and nutritional advice in other chapters of the book.


# PROFESSIONAL FOOTBALL ACADEMIES

Most professional football clubs have there own Academies, Development Centre's or Centre's of Excellence where they start training children from the age of 5-6 all in aid of them finding the next group of talented youngsters who will go all the way into the first team and get professional contracts.

A scout is a representative from the professional teams club who is paid by the club to look for new players will look for talented kids at Saturday training, Sunday matches, holiday and after school camps or hear about players from word of mouth. If they see a player they like then the scout should approach the club/team manager first (not the parents directly) who will then introduce the scout to the parent. The scout might just want to watch your child and see how they develop before asking if they would like to come along and train or invite them for a trial.

If there is a trial this can be a day training with lots of other children who have also been scouted. Hundreds of children get scouted year in year out and only a few make it in to the academy team, so its worth making sure your child understands that by getting picked for a trial doesn't mean they will definitely be getting into the academy, It can be a big disappointment if they're not prepared for this.

This process is different for each club, some clubs have two or three tiers within their academy, some children may go straight in at the top whereas others have to work their way up, some clubs train less days then others and where they train can be far away.

The Development Centre's or Academy coaches look out for certain skill sets that the childern should have which they then can develop more to make them a complete player.

As an example of this process, my son was scouted and invited to train at a championship club, he had to attend training 3 times a week on Mondays, Wednesdays, Fridays and then play a game on a Sunday. Training started at 4:45pm-6pm and you had to be there 15 minutes early at 4:30pm.

On Friday you were told about the game on Sunday. After six weeks he was assessed using a format they called SPIT (speed, personality, intelligence, technique). This assessment will vary from club to club. (This training process is something you can help your child with whether they're in a club or not. By getting them to learn the drills, skills and tecniques that are in this book and on my YouTube channel). After the six weeks you will either be offered a contract to join or released.

If you are successful, this process of assessment will continue at the club from time to time and if you fall behind or are not making improvements then you may get released or dropped into the development centre. This will continue all the way until you are offered a professional contract or released.

This can be a very harsh process for the children and parents because of the way the clubs tell the players, and because you both may have been going for many years only to be released. Some clubs will send you a letter and others sit you down and say that they aren't going to offer your child a contract with a list of reasons why.

As you can well imagine for young children under the age of 13 this is a difficult time, they may need help and support from family to get them back on the right track. This is also a good opportunity to remind them that they're very young and still have more years in which to develop their skills, intelligence and body-strength. Also reinforce to them that if they were good enough to get to a club in the first place then another club may take more of a chance with them.
If the club haven't given you any advice on what to do next then you should ask them what is it that your child can do to improve their football and chances of getting into a different club or back into this one.

For older children, now young adults, this rejection after their hopes have been built up can be potentially devastating. They may have given so much time and energy to a club and been on the verge of signing a professional contract but now are left with nothing. What happens now is the most important time in this young adults quest to be a footballer. Not only are they becoming an adult with very strong views on how things should be in the world, but they are also finding out what they want from life. Like relationships, jobs, money, a different career, party's with friends etc. etc. As a parent this time is also hard because you too have also invested a lot, including your time and money into following this footballing process of training and games over the years. Emotions will be running high and you may feel angered by what has happened take a little time out for you and your child to assess the other opportunities. For the younger children there is time to find out if they want to keep focusing on football or not, but for the older teenagers it's different their options are more limited becasue they maybe to old to get into another academy and will have to start thinking about a different career if they don't want to pursue professional football anymore.

## OTHER ACADEMIES AND DEVELOPMENT CENTRES

There are many other types of academies and development centres run by qualified FA coahces or ex professional footballers which are good, as they can teach the kids a lot of what they learned during their careers. Also they may still have connections to their old clubs, so getting trials or being able to talk to managers about players in their academies will be easier for them.
In these academies and development centres you will have to pay to go there, the prices will vary from centre to centre.
These centres may also do a weekend and summer scheme which is very good as other academies can be closed over the summer period.

They may not have the facilitates or lots of high level professional coaches but they are great because you get to play against other top academies and also professional academies. Also the ex professional coaches can give you more attention, like 1 on 1 training sessions harnessing on the specific details that you will need to make it in the professional game.

To find out about any of these academies, if you look on the internet or ask the manager at your club you'll be able to find one close to you or one that fits into your price range.

# DEVELOPMENT - BODY AND MIND

At the age of 5-9 your child will be just starting out playing so their development should be all about enjoyment playing fun games of football learning different kinds of basic skills using a ball whether it's heading, kicking or volleying getting them used to a ball.

Get them used to running with a ball, try and get them to use both feet if possible but don't pressure them if they can't. Also get them to try kick ups this will help loads to improve your child's touch. Start to tell them about calling for the ball and moving into spaces on the pitch. There are videos of football drills, skills and techniques in this book to help your child's development.

If they play for a team the coach will be teaching them theses things, but get them to practice at home as well.

Between the ages of 11-13 their football will become more serious and your child will also become more focused, this is a good time to get them to try more skills and learn the other side of football. Perfect what they have been practicing since the age of 5. Start to go more in depth about matches, finding the spaces on the pitch, what should they be thinking before they get the ball, team play, rejection, being on the bench and not being picked etc.

Watch matches on tv looking at why players do what they do. Your child will also start to develop muscles and start to grow at different rates so learning the physical side of the game is very important as well. Teach them about warming up and cooling down after training and matches. Stretching muscles and building up stamina these things will be essential in their development and will help them in their teenage years.

# TEENAGE YEARS

# ADULTHOOD AND DEVELOPING

This is a very important time not only in your quest to be a footballer but also in your life as a whole. Further to what was said in your youth years you are now becoming an adult and under going many physical and mental changes that will affect your life entirely. Knowing how to look after your body and mind at this time is important so you can develop properly, and then maintain this for the rest of your life. More important than playing football at this time is what you do off the field and the way you live your life that will have the greatest effect on your footballing career.

At the beginning of your teenage years your body will start to undergo many changes making you stronger and more socially aware of what you are doing. Things like peer pressure start to arise and you will also start to be more experimental, trying lots of new things from other sports to doing things that you weren't allowed to do before. This is where help, understanding, patience and guidance is needed form both parties, as most teenagers feel that they know best and mayn't want to listen to their parents or carers but instead are keen to test boundaries and push new limits making things emotionally highly strung between you & them.

The physical development from youth to adulthood will be different for each person, for some the process will be quicker with the bodies getting taller and stronger for others it will feel as if they haven't grown at all or developed any muscles/breasts yet these changes will happen to everyone in due course so don't panic. When these physical changes start to occurr you can start to train your muscles to get stronger and more flexible, but be careful not to over do it because you're still growing and have more chances of causing muscle damage, tears, dislocations or fracturing bones. There are some exercise drills and fitness plans in this book that will help you at this time. Your physical peak is around the ages of 21-29 so take your time building up your muscles before then.

Emotionally you'll be going through changes as well, so developing the mind is

essential. Brain training exercises that help the mind to react quicker will be great to help you in football because you need to get information and process it quickly in football.

Learn to deal with new emotions and hormones as best as you can during this time as there will be lots of trials and errors, triumphs and failures so try and treet both of them in the same way, don't get either too high or too low emotionally as the after effects can lead to rash decisions about your football career.


## LIFE OUTSIDE OF FOOTBALL

This is for me the most influential, testing and exciting times in your life.

As a young boy or girl at the ages of 2-11 you were learning new things all the time and developing skills to help you with that learning. But once you get to around 12 and through your teens you start learning about you and what you want to do with your life. From going to college or university which could be anywhere in the country or out of the country for that matter, to getting a job and starting on a path to a successful career. These are some of the things that will have a big effect on your footballing career or whether you want to become a footballer.

Some of the challenges you may have to overcome during this time include gangs, drugs, drinking or pregnancy. We have all heard of the teenage stroppy kid that doesn't clean or want to help around the house, is lazy and would rather chill with friends then get a job, eats everything you buy within the same day, starts to drink and smoke, may take drugs, plays computer all day and always has an answer for everything. But what some of us don't know is how to handle any of these situations without it spiralling out of control into something unmanageable leaving the young adult vulnerable to all kinds of problems that could result in mental heath issues and in worse cases suicide.

As a parent these times are testing and very hard, you may be a single parent trying to make ends meet and don't have the time you'd like to dedicate to your child or to even see if there is a problem until its too late. Your child maybe very secretive and not tell you everything about what they're doing, it could be drink, drugs or sex you won't know until its too late and no-one wants this to happen.

So as a teenager wanting to become a footballer you'll need to a think about how some activities you might want to do can affect your future like riding motor bikes, snowboarding and skate boarding things like these can be dangerous for you and can cause injuries. So be careful and if people tell you something worrying about your future then take note and think about it, they are only looking out for you, not trying to control you.

For parents at this stage in your child's life communication is the key, understanding is a little further down the list because sometimes your son or daughter will do things without understanding why they did them themselves saying "i don't know why i did it, i just felt like doing it." They maybe getting bullied by a partner into doing things they don't want to do. Domestic violence can happen even at a young age and be very subtle or it can be very violent and obvious to others. You may feel like you can't get away and feel trapped as many people who are going through things like these do. If you or anyone you know is going through this you can contact people in confidence and get help and support from companys like Yarna if you feel that you can't turn to your parents or maybe you don't have parents to turn to. So if your child does talk to you then you can start to address any situation that may occur, this maybe even looking to get outside help with some matters from people who know more about how to deal with these problems.

The other thing that is secondary only to communication is support. As a parent you will now have to give more support in what your child is going to do with their lives. Halfway through secondary school they will be making choices on what lessons to take which will be looking at what GCSE's they will then undergo. This decision should be done together and not just them or you alone, this is a good start for you both to get an understanding of how to approach future decisions like what collage or university to go to. But with each decision you as a parent should slowly be taking more of a back seat until your child now young adult is making the decisions themselves but with you supporting their decisions. If this process is done from a young age 11 or 12 and is jointly done until around 21 with the parent being less and less influential on the final decision from around 19, then you will both be confident that the decision they make would be something that you would both agree on.

For parents and youngsters going through this or soon to be going through this at some point always talk to each other letting each other know how you feel about things with friends, school, collage, partners etc. Let each other know that there is full support and that you're in these things together not alone.

## EDUCATION, WORK AND FOOTBALL

At this age if you're at an academy or development centre you will be mixing your education and training almost everyday and developing your skills. What will also help you as a player at this time is watching the 1st team train, and seeing how the players train with their manager or coach, as this is where you would like to be one day, and its great to know what kind of things you will be doing on a regular basis and the best ways to do them. Also you can speak to the older professionals and ex professionals who are still involved with the club as the experience they have is invaluable because they would have seen it all, been there, done that and got the t-shirt and still doing it at the club.

Even though you're in the academy to play football, and this is to be your main focus you should take your education very serious as well. You might think that you're going to get offered a contract but the possibilities are that 90% of you will have to look for another club or drop out into semi professional football and work or go to college. Leaving you a choice of whether to continue or not continue playing football.

If you're not in an academy or a development centre then you should be looking to play football at the highest level possible for you. If your in your early teens (13 to 15) then playing in a men's semi- professional team will be highly unlikely as in the semi-pro game the youngest 1st team players tend to be around 17 years old. If you go to a semi-professional club for a trial you may not get into the 1st team but they'll put you in the youth team or reserves which is still a shop window for you to be seen in, especially if you're doing well.

It's always good to have a back up plan or a plan B if football doesn't work out for you which in most cases it doesn't. So if you have another passion or something that you can see yourself doing in the future, then if at school choose your options wisely and learn all you can because you will be getting this education for free in secondary school. Once you leave it will cost you to be educated which will defiantly have an effect on your football as you may have to get a job to help fund your education. So it's quite good for you to get all the qualifications you can for free and have these things under your belt so you can do what you want with them, rather than chasing after them later on and paying loads and putting pressure on yourself to complete them.

If you are working part time or full time the main thing for you is to get as much training and matches in as possible. It may be hard for you to  find the time but make sure you do. Look at your schedule for a week or month and organise your training around that. There is a 12 week programme in this book and video drills made by professionals, ex-professionals and academy coaches to help you so you can organise your week without worrying about making up training sessions.

If you are working loads and making good money you may feel like football is becoming a secondary thing, don't feel pressured to pursue your football career because this can have a reverse effect, giving you undue stress in games and training. Also you may feel a bit tired from work both mentally and physically, this will also have an effect on your performance. If this is happening on a regular basics then you will need to revaluate your decisions as whether to stay in the game or carry on with your working career.

This is where you'll have to be as honest as you can with yourself as to what is the highest standard of football you'll be able to play in. Really take your time about this and speak to others in the game, family and friends but the choice should come down to you. Whatever choice you make stay as positive as you can always make your football as enjoyable as you can stay in love with the game until you feel there is nothing left, otherwise you'll regret the choice you've made.

## ACADEMIES AND DEVELOPMENT CENTRES

If you're in your late teens and in an academy then they will look to offer you a scholarship/pro or release you. This can be a terrible time for the ones that get released because you may have been at the academy for many years, sometimes from the age of 6 and now find yourself released with no club to go to feeling very let down like you want a break from it all and maybe never come back. For most people this can be demoralising and can even make them feel slightly depressed. It's easy for me to write things like "stay strong, be positive don't worry you'll get another team". To let you know from my own experiences and every footballer that's ever made it, we have all had knock backs like this and been told your useless, no good, you'll never make it, sent out on loan, released or dropped. I felt my club was stopping my move to a pro club and made a rash decision not to play for team again leaving the country to play in Sweden, in hindsight i could have stayed here and had another go with a different pro club.

If you play in an academy far away you may have to move away from home to a boarding school organised by the club to get your education as well as doing your football or if you're too old for school you'll be moving into digs (a place to live) with another footballer or with another family. Some may like this and others mayn't, missing home and their own families. Luckily in this day and age we have great forms of communication that can make it a little bit easier for you. But if you're having trouble then you should speak to your coach and explain how you feel as this may start to affect your football. Your club should try and help you with solving this problem by maybe letting you go home more times or arranging for family members to come and stay with you, whatever is needed to make you feel more at easy.

What you do off the pitch with your time is as important as what you do in the academy. Try and mix your time up by doing some days of extra training, gym sessions, ball work etc with relaxing times stretching, saunas etc and fun times with mates something to take your mind off football for little bit.
Development centres are made for the players that don't make it into academies or have been released by clubs. Some centres have scouts that look out for players that have been missed by these academies and take them on because they have seen something in a player that they like and think that with their training they'll be able to make that player better ready for their academy.

Most development centres are associated with the professional club so they can keep an eye on players incase they get better, they also play matches against other development centres. They're bigger in size than academies with hundreds of players in them and pro clubs have many of these centres around the country so not to miss any players from any area.
The training should be of a good standard but you should be always looking to develop yourself more by doing whatever extra you can. Ask your coach what they think you need to improve and start to practice that, also have what you want to improve on and add that to your practice, once you've praticed the other stuff first.

Just like the boys in academies your time off the pitch is just as important as on it. So again try to mix up your training just as they should with relaxed pastimes and different kind of training sessions. As before there are sessions and execerises in this book and on my YouTube channel to help you.

Interview with Harry Redknapp

Interview with Teddy Sheringham

One thing you'll need to do no matter whether you're in an academy, development centre or on your own is to find out what you're not good at or need help with and start training in that area. Footballers should always be developing and moving forward pushing themselves to the limit wanting to be the best they can be. You may not know how or what to improve so practice as many different things as you can. Practice is good but perfect practice makes perfect results, so don't do any sessions by half. Technique and quality beats unorthodox and quantity, give it your all and do the drills as best as you can even if you have to start slow and move on gradually.

## OPPORTUNITIES & REJECTION

One of the problems that occurs when your a teenager is getting the opportunity to play in important games where you can be seen by the people that matter. Or to play in men's teams, semi professional or 1st teams. Most of this is due to your physical development as these teams tend to pick physically bigger players feeling that they can held themselves better in the game.

There isn't much you can do about your size, as this is genetic. You can work on your strength to help you handle yourself in the step up from youth to senior football, there are drills on my Youtube channel to help you with this which have been tailored especially for teenagers during their growing stages so they don't injury themselves and cause problems.

What you can do which is defiantly in your hands is work on your football development e.g. Your ball control, ball skills, reading of the game, crossing, finishing and tackling depending on the position you play in. If you do this so you become the best player in your position not just in your team but in the whole club, you'll be knocking on the door of the 1st team without a doubt.

Your attitude is important as at this time may you feel like your team are only picking players they like or who are just big and not as good as you, that they aren't giving you a chance and that you hate being there and don't want to train anymore.

This won't help you in anyway. What will, is playing well and enjoying your football. The attitude you should have is to continue training well and hard, showing that you are willing to work hard to earn your place in the 1st team. By doing this you'll have more focus, play well and develop a stronger character which is what you need to be a footballer.

At this time play as many matches as you can. It doesn't matter what team you play in whether it's the youth team, 21s, reserve or 1st team playing matches puts you in the shop window the place to be seen by your manager, other managers and scouts. So if you are playing well then you'll be seen and wanted by whoever is watching this maybe your manager or another teams manager, But not playing can lead to wanting to leave, hating your football, losing your confidence, losing your touch and skills which means that in training you'll have to work even harder to make sure that you are keeping up your match fitness your focus and skill level.

So if anything like this happens, grit your teeth take it on the chin and stay in the game. But if you really can't take it anymore rather than getting upset and feeling down arrange to speak to the manager and tell him what you feel don't hold anything back as the more open and honest you are the more that you'll both understand where you are and what can help you even if that means to leave the club.

Rejection is something in football that will occur a few times, this will happen to some more then others. But don't think that it only happens to you and that others can do the same thing as you but get away with it making you feel like you've been picked on. It's not a nice thing to be rejected and it can be hard to swallow. Take your rejection as a learning opportunity, ask why you have been rejected and what can be done to improve yourself. Hopefully your manager or coach should tell you, if they don't this can be confusing and it's also a cop-out as they should be able to tell you something even if it's that, your not exactly what there looking for. Then get to it don't dwell on it too much start the healing process as soon as possible.

Another thing you could do is go into other sport using what you have learned from football. As I said before this is where your education is important and will put you ahead of others who haven't put in the work off the field that you have. If you can look at your rejections like this, one they'll be much easy to take and two you'll know where your going wrong especially if you keep hearing the same thing from different managers and coaches. Move on from your rejections as quickly as possible and get back to focusing on your football and enjoying yourself. If you feel that you need to talk to someone about how you feel, then do so. Don't hold things in get it out and clear your head. Also talking to someone and getting a different point of view maybe just what you need, as this may make you see things in a different light or more clearly.

## OTHER JOBS THAT YOU CAN DO, IF FOOTBALL DOESN'T WORK OUT

You may have been knocking at the football door for a long while now, even had a few opportunities at academies been a second year scholar, you may even have signed a professional deal and dropped out having only been in the 21s. Whatever it is if you have done your education right then many doors can be opened for you to go into, if you have decided not to carry on pursuing you football career, below are a few career ideas:

Online and social media could be an alternative platform to showcase your talent and get paid. You could make film content about football or sport in your own way from making your own versions of advertisements to presenting your own sports show like the F2 or Dude perfect. The opportunity is there for you, all you would need to do is be as creative as you can and get a good team behind you.
You can also get in contact with people in and around your favourite club or a club that you would like to work for and ask them about maybe making their website, updating their website or doing their sports media marketing. This will work better with the lower league clubs than the bigger clubs but don't be afraid to try any club that you choose. (Contact their HR department, social media department)
If you've been registered with the PFA then you can speak to them about what options you have through them, you could do your coaching badges with them

as coaching is an obvious choice. You can coach at many levels, from under 7 all the way up to men's and women's football you can also do more specific coaching like goal keeping or striker's coaching. The badges you'll need to get are your level 1, level 2(uefa B) and level 3 (uefa A) etc. Management will take a few years to complete so the sooner you start the sooner you'll finish and the longer you'll have to be a manager.

Sports science is becoming more important and more widely used in sport today and football is starting to join in, so going down this road will also be a good option for you. Once again you'll also need to get qualifications to do this which also takes a few years to complete depending on what level you want to go to.

The same can be said for stats so if you develop a new way of keeping stats in games or have lots of stats stored on a database for people to use the bigger your company will be like Opta, or you could aplpy to work for them.

*"Trying is the key to success. Only by trying something many times over will you not only perfect it, but more importantly know how you got it wrong. So try and fail until you succeed"*

## Dean Holness: Southend United

# SEMI-PROFESSIONAL FOOTBALL

# THE SEMI-PROFESSIONAL GAME

The semi-professional football scene is a high level of football with some good players and teams, some with a good following of football loving fans. Teams can get a couple of thousand supporters turning up to watch, especially if the nearest big professional club is playing away. This can feel quite special to players new to this level of football especially when you play well and score the winning goal in a match watched by a big crowd of fans.

Some semi-professional clubs are more like League 2 professional clubs especially ones in the Conference Premier. Training around 4 times a week with players on the same or higher wages then players in League 2, this does tend to be the minority though and is not the norm. Most don't have these luxuries and struggle to pay wages and sadly don't have many supporters. But if it is football you are interested in rather than the lifestyle or just to be called a footballer then this is a good place to be for a teenager trying to break into the professional game.

More then likely if you are playing at this level then you would either have a job or go to college to get a qualification and a career, so you'll have to decide whether your football revolves around your work/studies or your work/studies revolves around your football. This is a choice you will have to make yourself have a talk with your family, close friends or relations because it can depend on the job your doing or the length of time your studying that will be major factors in your decision.

The semi professional level of football maybe the highest level that some players ever get to, they may be lucky to have a long career there, playing 13+ years enjoying their football and making extra money on top of their normal jobs, with no pressure unlike some lower league professionals who only have football and no other income. If you are wise you can use this extra income to generate even more cash by investing it or use it to enjoy life like pay for holidays etc.

For those few still keen to progress beyond this level it's the best place to get spotted by professional clubs whose scouts go there looking for young exciting talented players to get at a cheap price hoping they have uncovered a gem. For me semi-professional football is best when teams play talented youngsters mixed with a few older players or ex professionals. This is good for the young players to get 1st team experience playing in front of crowds in important matches. They can also learn from the ex professionals who have been in the game for many years and have great knowledge and experience from playing at a higher level or the highest level of football.

If you win the Conference Premier league you get promoted into the professional leagues lowest division, which is League 2. This drives all the teams in that league to fight for promotion. If the youth and enthusiasm is mixed with the experience and know how to win matches this is can be an exciting, passionate and very competitive league to be in and also watch.

## HOW TO GET INTO SEMI PROFESSIONAL FOOTBALL

There are different routes into the semi professional game but not as many as the professional game, you can't get scouted as semi professional clubs don't really have scouts because they can't afford to pay them but you can be recommended by someone. You may still need to do a trial and attend training sessions play a few games in the reserves. You can find out where your nearest semi professional club is and ask the manager/reserve team manager if you can come on trial. An agent can also help you get straight into the team or on trial as they have many contacts and may know a few managers personally.

Most but not all semi-professional clubs have a youth team which is usually run from ages of 15+ so if you are young enough to player for one of these teams then that's a good place to be because it will be easier to get into the reserve and first team from there. Pre season is a good time to ask for a trial at semi pro clubs so contact the one you would like to play for and see if you can go in then.

If this is the highest level that you get to then don't feel too upset about not making it into the professional game. After all football is about doing the best you can, enjoying yourself, competing to win matches, tournaments and leagues which is what you will be doing when playing semi professionally.

If you have been released by a professional club or academy/development Centre you should be looking to get into another professional club or academy first, but if this isn't possible then the next place you should be looking is at the semi professional level.

There will be teams near you, which may be looking for players, and if you have been at a professional club or one of these academies Centre's then it will be easier for you to get into a semi professional club or at least for a trial.

Look to play for a club that plays football to suit your style of play, you can find this out by going to watch them or if you get a trial you'll know while your at training. It wouldn't be beneficial to your development to go to a team that plays long ball football if you are a small tricky midfielder even if they are paying the most wages as you mayn't play many games or will have to change your style of football to fit in the team. This could jeopardize your chances of making it back into the professional game.

If you're young and haven't made it into a professional club yet and are ready to progress to the semi professional game then you need to find a team that has young players in the first team as this means that they are more likely to give youngsters a chance. There may only be one or two clubs in your area and these may not play a lot of youngsters, if this is the case then you will need to knuckle down and work even harder at training and in games (reserve and friendly matches) to get yourself recognized and into the first team. This may take a while but stay positive, focused and happy, and your chance will come.

Once you do get into a semi professional club and are playing well they may ask

*"First of all love the game, secondly be able to deal with knock backs being dropped, injured or released and have the ability to come back stronger"*

## Paul Davis: Arsenal & England International

*"Love the game because if you don't you won't survive."*

## Martin Keown: Arsenal & England International

*"Always make sure that you are early for training. Don't give anyone the excuse that you don't want it enough."*

## Sagi Burton: Crystal Palace, Port Vale & Peterborough United

*"Hard work beats ability every time. You need both but to apply your ability you need the hard work first"*

## James Evans: Tottenham Hotspurs & Bristol City

you to sign a contract offering you wages and a regular place in the first team. This maybe your first contract and you may feel overjoyed at being offered one. However don't be pressured into signing something that you don't know much about.

If you are young and looking to step up to a higher level it would be best to get someone with a knowledge of contracts to have a look before signing or if you can speak to an agent (if you have one). The reason you are doing this is so that you don't sign your life away or get stuck in the future incase you want to leave or if a bigger club comes in for you and somehow you can't leave because of a contractual problem. Contracts are very complicated things, made to look easy so my advice is to leave the contacts to the people who deal with them regularly and the football to you.

## TRAINING

The average semi professional player will train at least two times a week and play games on Saturdays. Some players will have jobs, families, college or other commitments they have to take into consideration when playing at this level.
This can make it hard for them to do what is needed to be done if you want to progress to a higher level of football.
You should be training around four times week, alternating from gym workouts to football drills in order to get your body and mind heading towards their peaks. By doing this your level of football will increase.

You'll need to fit your training around your life outside of football, work or college. You'll need to fit in at least two extra sessions per week; you should already be training on a Tuesday and Thursday night, (the average semi professional club normally trains on these days.) This will leave you a Monday, Wednesday, Friday and Sunday you will need to leave a day to two of rest in there. An example week could look like this: Monday -gym, Tuesday-Training, Wednesday-gym,

Thursday-Training, Friday -rest, Saturday-game, Sunday- rest.

Every so often try to fit in a yoga or Pilates session on one of your gym days, as this will help the body to be strong and flexible, stretching is just as important as the exercise. This will take a lot dedication as you may need to train at times when you'll be tired or when you don't won't to, but this will be the difference between those who want it, and those who really want it. Those who want it will make excuses and not train and those who really want it will train without excuses. Those will be the most likely ones to succeed (you make your choice). Ask players in your team if there is anywhere you can get extra training. They may know of another club in a different league that has good facilities where you can use the gym or maybe a pitch where you can practice football and fitness drills. Some players may want to do it with you, training together can make you train harder then when your doing it by yourself.

Eating like a professional athlete will help as it will get the body ready to perform all the physical demands that you're going to ask of it and have the ability to recover and do it again tomorrow. Once you start doing this and having the mindset of a professional athlete, it will become easier to do and you will improve.
There are some meal plans in the nutrition chapter.

## FITTING IN

Like professional football the semi professional game will have managers and chairmen looking out for the club's best interests and players looking out for their own interests. Sometimes it may feel like there are people that you're not connecting with stopping you from playing football the way you want to. You may have feelings of not being wanted, this can be detrimental to your game. This feeling can sometimes be because you may be new to the club and have yet to gel with the other players, with most of them already being great friends. Or you may not be playing as many games as you wish putting the blame on not fitting in with the team. If you feel like this you need to talk with your manager he should then be trying to make you feel more at ease, especially if he values you and wants you to stay at the club. This maybe by telling you that you're wanted at the club or it may open up the discussion as to whether it is best for you to start looking for another club. So when you arrive at a club start to settle yourself in as soon as possible, make friends and be yourself but most of all let your football do as much talking as possible..

This feeling of not fitting in or being unsettled can also happen off the pitch and stem from moving home or family problems. If this happens you may need to talk to someone else rather than your manager, someone close to you as this matter maybe very personal. Its not a problem or a disgrace to go and get counselling for help in any matter that you find is bringing you down. Unsettled and clouded visions make people react in funny ways and can make you do things that you wouldn't normally do, sometimes leading you down roads which you don't want to really be going down. If you are unhappy off the pitch the chances are that you'll be terrible on the pitch, as a player who isn't focused is no good to anyone including himself or herself and nobody wants that.

Try and find happiness, just PLAY your football, try to enjoy it, whatever team you are in 1st, reserves, youth team or even just at training.

In training try new skills, tricks, passing and shooting techniques, don't worry about making mistakes trying something new is better then never trying at all. Since being a baby you've been trying things and not giving up, so don't start holding yourself back now. Remember mistakes will be made and lessons will be learned, repeat this over and over to yourself and soon you will find that you make fewer mistakes and have learned loads.

Football is all about choices and decision making when to pass, when to shoot etc. When you are playing well these choices become easy and you don't even seem to think of them. But when your not playing well, things seem that much harder and play on your mind. When you are trying too hard, your body becomes tense and your mind is not clear this makes you not play not like yourself.

Try and relax yourself and play your way back into your football, work hard off the ball and keep things simple to start with, once you have got a feel for the game again then you will start to relax and play the game the way you want to.

You will come across many crossroads in your football career and the right direction may not always be clear and easy to see but if your positive, decisive, and don't faulter from your aim then things will be a lot easier to see.

## PROGRESSING TO THE NEXT LEVEL

Trying to progress higher into the professional game maybe difficult from here because of your age or because of an old injury. You may have been released from a professional club and now have a sour taste in your month about the professional game or you may now have to look after your new family or have a day job you really like and are happy to play semi professionally picking up extra money still playing a really good standard of football. Maybe you don't want the pressure of being a professional footballer, there is nothing wrong with wanting to play at this level and working in a job that you like. Happiness is always the key.

If you do want to progress to the professional leagues then you need to start with always playing in the first team, this is your first priority. Then you need to be making a lot of noise. I.e. you are playing so well in games that other teams in the semi professional leagues are hearing about you and want you playing for them not against them. You'll also be getting yourself in the non-league newspaper all the time which is where managers, scouts and agents all look if your name keeps popping up then they'll come to you. An agent can help you make it to the next step as they have the right connections, unfortunately it's not always about your talent, and it can sometimes be all about who you know. To find out more about agents look at the agent's chapter.

Don't just accept the first offer that comes your way, as you may already be in a better situation by getting good money and playing the kind of football that you love. Assess all the areas and then find the best outcome for you. (Remember everybody is different and what works for some may not work for you, listen to what people have to say but the final decision will be all yours.

Going on trial is another way of getting into a professional game, be careful about going on too many trials as this can hinder your future, teams will soon get to know your name and that you've been on trial here, there and everywhere. They may wonder why you haven't stayed at these clubs. Also going on so many trials can be very demoralizing if you keep getting rejected. Being fit is really important if you want to make the step up, teams want to take on new players that they can play in the team straight away rather then have to wait till they get fit which could take any amount of time.

## MAKING THE RIGHT CHOICES FOR YOUR FUTURE

If you are 28 and over, the likelihood of making it into the professional game is very higly unlikely. If you fall into the 28 and over bracket then you'll need to think about your future and staying in semi professional football. From here you can now start to think about life after football for example you may want to go into managing, coaching, youth team management or being an agent etc.. If you want to leave football altogether and purse working in your current job whatever your decision you will want to look back at your footballing career with no regrets.

You'll have had many ups and downs, made some great friends along the way and enjoyed many laughs. There is no other kind of life then forfilling the one you've dreamed of doing since you was a child. Give back what you can, pass on your knowledge to youngsters and look forward to your future.

Here is an interview I did with professional footballer Jamie Cureton while he was playing for Dagenham & Redbridge FC giving advice on how to get into the professional game.

Interview with Jamie Cureton

*"enjoy your football, practice - practice - practice and don't be afraid to try things, be a willing learner and have the right attitude and enthusiasm....many are called but few are chosen".*

## Carl Leaburn: Charlton Athletic & Wimbledon

*"Managers don't like people who don't give any effort, slackers. Skills sometimes don't come off but hard work always works".*

## Marc Bircham: Millwaill, QPR & first team coach at QPR

*"Dedication, work hard and practice even when others don't want to. From a managers point of view, players should have all these attributes and have a great attitude towards wanting to be a footballer."*

## Harry Redknapp: Tottenham & West Ham Utd manager

*"Sacrifice and dedication. Practicing when your mates are going out drinking and partying."*

## Teddy Sheringham: Millwall, Tottenham & Manchester United

# WOMENS FOOTBALL

From the age of 6 until 16 girls and boys can play football in the same teams the development and training is pretty much the same at the age of 6 but when you get to the teenage years the physical side changes dramatically. Which is maybe a good time to start lookng for an all girls team. You can find local teams in your area by looking online.

It's around the 13 year old mark that these things start to happen due to hormones and puberty boys start to become men and girls start to become women.

The fans divide also starts to happen here the mens game takes off where as the womens game starts to drop.

The gulf between the mens game and womens game is very visible once they become professionals. The women's game doesn't have the financial backing that the men's game does, so professional ladies don't make as much money as the men do, plus the endorsement deals are geared to the mens teams especially in the premier league.

The difference is huge in England compared to other countries in fact the highest paid female player in England in the year 2016 earned under £75k a year, which included endorsement deals. Compare that to the USA where the highest paid player made just under £2m and in Sweden they can earn up to £200k. So unless you play for one of the big teams here in England (even if your are) you may have to have another job as well to make enough money to have a good standard of living, especially if you live in London.

The top leagues in England are now called the FA WSL 1, FA WSL 2; the big teams play in the FA WSL 1. The youth teams/scholarships and development centres, FA player development, advance coaching centres and centres of excellences are all places where you can play and develop yourself trying to become a top flight player. They are also the best places to be in if you want to get scouted by one of the top flight teams.

Compare this to teams in other countries like the USA, Sweden and Asia where there is a bigger emphasis on women's football then the appeal would be to go abroad and try your luck there. But the English game will soon follow in the footsteps of these other countries especially as in the 2015 World Cup the England women's team came 3rd, with 1,353,506 people attending the matches (26,029 per match) and millions watching, it will only be a matter or time.

To learn how you can get yourself into one of these scholarships schools or development centres take a look on the FA website who head women's football in England.

The most important thing that I can say is to love the game as there will be many testing times ahead on and off the field, so as well as being physically fit and strong you'll need to be mentally fit and strong.

FA Womens Website

I interviewed West Ham United girls U10s manager Greg Regan about the shape of womens football in England from grass roots to professional.

1, How much does the average women's professional get paid?
Not much! WSL teams can pay 4 players over 12k per year, so basically a few teams had 4 pros at the club and the rest were semi-pro. Also foreign players will get paid a fair bit more. Arsenal were the 1st English team to pay players. A lot used to get given jobs by the club when they were not playing.

2, Do they work other jobs?
Most will have. An England player who played in the 2015 World Cup works part-time at Deutche Bank. She had 2 ACL's (ligament injury) so needed a job when injured. Most players in the Top English division are not full time.

3, Is there academy schools? and for what ages?
30 Centre of Excellences (COE's) in England. Receive funding from FA U9-U17s. In London for example the COEs are Arsenal, Millwall, Chelsea & Middlesex FA. COE's only play against each other. They train twice a week for 4hrs total. West Ham, Spurs & Charlton are not COE's and compete in 'local' grassroots leagues.

4, Is there a semi professional level?
Most WSL 1 & 2 players will be semi-pro. Below that the odd club might pay some expenses. No one at West Ham Ladies is paid. One player travels 1 and a half hours to training twice a week.

5, How hard is it to get a scholarship? and what do you need to get one?
There are companies that do trials and are linked to US colleges. One of the West Ham Ladies players is off to America for a scholarship.

6, What country's are good for women's football?
For me Germany best league and team. France have 2 pro teams (Lyon & PSG) who are very strong and a strong national team. PSG v Lyon is the Champions League final 2017.
I expect either Germany, France or USA to generally win the World Cup. Japan are also good very technical.

7, How hard is it going through puberty and playing football?
Not an expert here. I do have parents text me saying their daughter didn't play well cos of PMT though! Probably something male coaches need to take into consideration more.

8, Like most sports football is emotionally high, is there a significant change in womens dressing rooms compared to mens?
Only been involved with young age groups so can't really comment. Julian Dicks always describes womens football as like men's but without the egos. He manages the 1st team at West Ham United.

9, What do you think would help women footballers and young girls wanting to become footballers?
More role models, more girls football in schools, Futsal for girls. I run sessions. Men's teams supporting womens football more, more tv coverage, more professional teams which will raise the standard and make it more marketable for tv.

# TRIALS

# A LITTLE INFO

When on trial at any club it's hard to know exactly what the manager will be looking for and as each manager is different they will all be looking for different things in a player. But there are somethings that all managers would love to see in a player is that unique spark or talent that sets them aside from all the other players and is clear to all watching. That something which can't be taught lighting pace, immense physical strength, amazing skill, six sense like awareness giving you the ability to read the game better than anyone else.

But if you don't have these things you'll have to get noticed and make an impression in a different way. By showing that your not scared of the trial, always wanting the ball and never giving up.

If you don't get pick to stay on it could be because of many things, but most of all it's about opinions, and people all have different opinions on what kind of player they think is good. So you mayn't fit into this one but might fit in the next one.

# WHAT TO DO ON A TRIAL

## YOUTHS:

When you are young (around 6-13yrs old) you will find that you are doing lots of trials at many different teams from school to district, league teams and academies. So you will be seeing new players and new coaches all the time. You'll also be dealing with achievement and rejection because of this. Parents/Carers will need to be very supportive around this time and not pushy as your child maybe the one that gets rejected and my already be feeling bad about themselves, which is where I'd suggest giving them some time out from trials and let them play football with their team or friends and practice a few more techniques, before trying to put them on trial again.

Introduce yourslef, get to know the names of the people your trialing with, socialize as this could be the team that you will be playing for and you'll want to get on

61

with the other players as quickly as possible. The quicker you settle in the quicker you can enjoy your football and the trial your having.

If in a match ask for the ball all the time even if you've already made a mistake in the game, this will show you have character and that you are willing to keep trying, it will also help you get into the game. Get on the ball loads this will help you put your stamp on the game, and give your team confidence in you and confidence in yourself.

Know your favourite position/positions that you play in because you maybe asked where you play and if you don't have an answer then you'll be put in a position that you don't often play in or whatever position is left, leaving you already worried about the trial match before you've even started it.

Try your best but don't over do it and deliberately be greedy by not passing the ball to others and keeping it to yourself, this may have a reverse effect as it may look like exactly what it is, that your trying to hard and not capable of making the right decisions.

TEENAGERS:
For older trialists: (14 and upwards) going on trial will be a lot different. First of all your fitness will play a big part in your trial. If you are going on a semi professional or professional trial most the team will have a certain level of fitness and you will need to be at that level or higher to stand a chance, so get your fitness up to its best before even going on trial.

Know the best position that you play in, introduce yourself to the team. Many of the players will already know each other and may have formed a great friendship. It may seem as though your on the outside but by being friendly and social you will find your trial easier and more enjoyable.

Be relaxed about the whole trial, you may find yourself getting very nervous about going on trial and during your trial which is understandable, but this will make you ether try too hard to please everyone or to nervous to try something incase you make a mistake. Which is the opposite of what you want to be doing. You should be excited and relaxed, free to be yourself,

*"Practice, work hard and listen to your coaches, you can't go wrong with that."*

## Hayden Mullins: Crystal Palace, QPR & Birmingham City

*"Work hard, believe in your ability and also try to improve every day."*

## Mark Hall: Southend United & Torquay United

*"set small goals and when they have been reached set some more and when they have been reached set some again"*

## Hussein Isa: QPR Academy Coach

*" Love the game, Enjoy the journey, and know it will be a combination of your S.A.S (Skill, Attitude, Speed) that will determine the level you achieve in your career"*

## Richard Philpsy: Peterborough United

express your football and personality on and off the pitch.

Lastly days before the trial don't think too much about it and the outcome because this could affect you emotionally and physically, becasue if the outcome isn't what you want to hear then rejection will be harder to take making you feel even worse, which is not what you want. What you want is to feel that you prepared yourself well and gave it everything you got.

Enjoy your time and if you don't get in then learn form your time there and why you didn't get in.

## WHAT NOT TO DO ON A TRIAL

### YOUTHS:

Don't get worried about the trial, as whether you get in or not you'll have many years to improve your skills and start to become the player you want to be.

Normally trials at this age will be done by playing matches and will have a few training sessions thrown in, a really good thing to do is to try and not be shy, you will be new to the team and there maybe lots of other trialists there all wanting to make a good impression. So if you just shy away from things it may look as if this trial is over whelming for you or that you don't fit in.

Don't look at what others have got and what you don't, from their clothing like flash boots and all the latest gear to their skills, strength and speed. Concentrate on yourself and all the things that you have, because this is why you were chosen and is the foundation of your football the start of all things positive.

As you will be going to school and training you wouldn't have much time to juggle so don't leave your homework till the last minute. Get it done first so you leave as much time as you can to rest and look forward to your trial.

64

## TEENAGERS:

Don't be afraid to have the ball and try your skills even if you lose it or if they don't come off trying and failing is better then never trying at all.

Also if you don't want the ball it can look like you or hiding or playing out of your league, however it's seems you'll get over looked by the manager. This doesn't mean that you should be greedy and not pass the ball to anyone as players may do the same to you because they know that you won't give it back. Also the longer you keep the ball the more chance you'll have of losing it and making the same mistake over and over again.

Don't let your nerves get the better of you, try to calm your nerves and relax your-self, adrenaline will be pumping and emotions maybe high which may tense your body and stop you thinking freely. The best frame of mind and feeling you can be in to play a game of football is relaxed and focused.

Try not to be too focused as this can also make you tense. Also make sure your not too relaxed as you can become complacent and find it hard to rise your game if it's not going well.

Don't go on trial to any club knowing that you are about 70-80% fit and healthy because you won't be able to give it all you've got, you want to be able to show them your best and show them that you can get into the team straight away, also the other players will be fit and you'll stick out like a sore thumb.

Don't show off, be pigheaded or think that your better then everyone. The players and managers may not like it, you want to be able to work with these people once you get in.

## HOW TO GET A TRIAL

There are many different ways in which you can get a trial from the old fashioned way of writing to clubs, to the more modern way of sending in a video of you playing.

The best option is to be playing football for a club and to be playing well, scouts are at more games then you think and so are agents. These 2 sets of people can help you more than you realize and as they have connections to many different clubs at all levels of football.

Players in the club you're at may have connections to other clubs and can get you a trial their so asking your team mates can also be an option.

Another way would be to look on teams websites and contact their head scout or recuirtment team and ask when their trials are.

Most trials will be done during the pre-season period as teams have lots of friendly matches so the managers can start trying to sort out their team for the new season. In the months prior to pre-season you should be busy looking at what team you would like to play for and contact them. If your 1st choice isn't possible then you should try the team next down the line for you, so make a list of teams and slowly go through them until you get a trial.

If you don't get one then you should be looking to get into any team (if you aren't already) and start performing well so you can build up a good portfolio of yourself to send out for the next season.

Interview with Daniel Webb                    Interview with Paul Davis

66

# ADVICE FOR PARENTS / CARERS

# THE BUSINESS OF FOOTBALL

The idea of football being a job with the opportunity to make lots of money, a great lifestyle, travel the world, be idealized and have things that most people dream about is something that some people don't fully understand especially when compared to other sports, questions and comments often arise like "Why do footballers get so much money?" "They're so young and all they do is kick a ball around." The truth is that football over many years has become a business and one of the biggest money making businesses in the world. Everybody wants a bit of it whether it's television companies fighting over the rights to show the games to agents wanting ridiculous amounts of money for their players to be transferred from club to club. The clubs themselves making record profits year in year out, also moving their training schedules and locations to fit in with the new sponsorship deals, which is reaching out to ever growing consumers around the world, money, money, money.

When your in business what counts the most is how much money you're making and how much profit you can turn over. So for example when you're at work and your boss says "we need to find something that will boost our turn over and give us creditability". You say "if we pay £1 million a year and get John to join our team, he will generate us a turnover of £4 million giving us a profit of £3 million that same year". I'm sure your boss will be very happy.

This is what happens in football when a team buys a player, the team will also think about what that player can bring to them off the field through shirts sales, image rights, tickets and that gets bigger once you add sponsorship deals, television rights and winning trophies.

The problem with this is that the people who pay in the end are always the customers (the fans) having to buy the new television subscriptions to watch their team. The growing tickets prices, the new team shirts each year, etc etc.

But business is business and your not forced to buy the tickets or new shirts the teams will say. TV companies will say you don't have to buy the new subscriptions.

The people in the business are used at the businesses request, so if your not making the company money then your out the door. It's the same for the players if their not performing and winning games and trophies then there shown the door. Just like in business it's cut throat, contracts now mean almost nothing. At the highest level of football players and managers sign 5 year deals and leave within 2 years the loyalty is fading and will continue as long as the business side of football keeps growing.

Football is a law unto itself the rules are made up by the people involved in it like Knights of the Round Table. Once your in the circle it's great but being on the outside isn't enjoyable and is a place where players can crack, wanting to leave the club or football altogether. Some people can get slightly depressed or develop full depression wanting to do themselves or others harm. Being used like this is something that football needs to look at becasue the players are getting younger, the wages higher, lack of support never changing and the waste bucket bigger.

## HOW CAN I HELP MY CHILD?

One of the main things that you'll be needed for isn't that exciting but is the most important and that is to get them around for training to matches during the week and on the weekend. This will slowly feel like you're a mini cab service and that you don't have the time to do anything for yourself in the week or weekends anymore, and when your freezing yourself on the sidelines it may leave you feeling like let's leave next week out.
A few ways in which you can easy the burden of this is to ask a few parents to come together and take it in turns to take the kids to football, if not try and share it with your partner, grandparents or a friend someone who can take them once a month or fortnight so that you can do what you need to for yourself.

For yourself when you go to matches invest in a warm coat, thermals, gloves, hat, the works as it's always colder then what you think on the sidelines warmth over style.

Try and be at as many matches as you can because your child will love the fact that you're there and will remember it for life. Another thing is support, encouragement, listening and understanding at all ages in your child's life from the start all the way through their teens and on.

## SUPPORT

Be their biggest fan watching them develop into whatever player they end up being or even if they decide not to keep playing football.

Remember football is a matter of opinions and everyone has a different one. Some managers and coaches will think that your child isn't what their looking for, or they want to play them in a different position from the one you think they should play. Where's another manager will think your child's magic and wants them to be the key to the team. It will be hard but try and treat both these situations the same don't get big headed or too angry, because you child will certainly do that for you especially as a teenager. When they're younger it may be you who lets your emotions get the better of you, you'll need to be more level handed and the rock for your child to lean on, take whoever it is aside and talk to them.

Knockbacks are part and parcel of football and not easy to take, if you can give the right support to your child it'll be easier for your child to take and you can turn that around into a positive thing. For example your child has just been released by an academy after being there for years or not, they feel demoralised and so may you. You may leave and get into another academy or semi professional club putting your child right back in the game and back on track. But if they leave and do nothing because of the knockback, they will defiantly be out of the shop window with no chance of some other club picking them.
So you have to be strong for them and show them that we all get knockbacks, its how we recover that matters.

70

## ENCOURAGEMENT

Praise them when they feel down, encourage them when they feel like quitting and tell them how good they are when they do well.

The hardest part is to give them constructive criticism. So I think a good way to do this is to not criticise them at all about what they are doing or did wrong, but to tell them how they can improve on it., and if you can show them how to improve then that will help even more. If you can't get someone elss who can to show them.

In football your child should always be learning even if they manage to get to the very very top and play for their country, every game is different and will require a different aspect from them. It maybe something physical like strength, speed or aggression. It maybe mental like concentrating for 90 minutes, keeping focused on a specific strategy or adding something more to their game like heading better, playing with their weaker foot, free kicks, crosses, one on ones etc. If you can tell this to your child and yourself when the game hasn't gone their way or when the skills they've tried didn't come off, this will make those situations more positive rather than negative. e.g "you had lots some shots today son and was unlucky you didn't score, but that's how it goes sometimes. if you want we can practices some shooting another day"

This will help with your child and make them want to improve giving them the desire to achieve more.

## LISTENING

It's easy for parents to give encouragement, advice or criticism whether it's constructive or not but to listen to your child is something that doesn't come that easy, after all parents are there to raise, guide and teach their child/children the values of life as they see it. But listerning will help you and your child especially

71

*"When you don't have the ball your brain should be doing the talking, when you have the ball let your feet do the talking."*

*"It is great to have all the tricks and skills but what will make you a good player is, doing the basics things amazingly well and improving your knowledge of the game."*

*"Be fearless, try all the things that you have practiced in training. Sometimes they won't come off and you will get shouted out but don't let anything stop you trying again and again."*

*"Have a strong mental attitude. You need to be thick skinned, single minded & focused to get as far as you can in football"*

**Dean Holness: Southend United**

73

when they're teenagers. The problems they'll face and issues they'll have in training, matches, trials and in general will only be that much harder for them if they aren't able to let out some frustrations or tell someone how they really feel about the game or themselves. Just talking about it can ease a little pressure and relax them, which in some cases is all they needed.

When they're young it's not much of a problem, but it's the best time to start practicing so you can both get used to it, making it easier for when thet get older. But when they get to teenagers many things can happen from giving up all together to drinking, smoking, partying and turning to others instead of you because they feel that they can't talk to you anymore saying "you don't listen to me, all you do is tell me what to do and shout at me". This is something you don't want as in football there are too many ups and downs to take on alone and sharing the load makes it easier and better for both of you.

They'll be many conversations on the way to and from training/matches but at a young age try and limit the amount of conversations you have about them playing or how they've been playing as this will make them feel like every time they get in the car on the way to football your going to tell them ether what to do, how to play or what not to do. But if they bring it up themselves then keep it short and sweet.

When they're becoming teenagers and all their hormones are changing, times can become difficult and new boundaries will be tested. As a parent myself to 2 teenagers I have changed my parenting skills from 100% parent to 80% parent 20% best friend, this has worked out well for me and our conversations are easier becasue we feel more open and they feel that they can also tell me things about what their feeling and doing.

Once again this will help them massively with thier football career especially with the choice of whether to stay chasing the dream or look for another career around football.

Making them feel that your 100% behind them whatever decision they make.

## UNDERSTANDING

This is mainly understanding that all the choices made by your child whether a youth, teenager or in their 20s the final decision should be down to them.

When they're young football should be about fun and developing themselves, match results should be way down the list, but your child will want to have fun and win games. Remind them that you're happy as long as they enjoyed themselves and learn something new from the game whether it was individual, as part of a team or form the opposition. Ask them "did you have fun?" "did you learn anything?."

At a young age 5-9 you'll sometimes get some funny answers back and some really intelligent answers, don't worry too much about the answers the fact that your child can express themselves to you is a great start to the whole relationship and bonding process.

As teenagers the choices will be much different the results start to matter and the decisions become more difficult, and aren't just limited to the playing field. The kind of things that you'll come up against are them being on the bench a lot, managers using them as bit part players, stopping there development on the field, them wanting to go out with friends, having girlfriends/boyfriends, wanting to quit, etc. The disappointments also mean so much more losing games starts to hurt them, being told their no good at something or being released by clubs can easily take its toll on them. So the rock parent/friend that you are will put them in good stead to continue on. Don't let your own feelings and emotions take over you and in fluence your decisions on how to help. Take 5 and think about the situation properly, deal with it, then move on.

## WHAT TO EXPECT FROM YOUR CHILD AND FOOTBALL

Don't expect anything from football, it doesn't owe you or your son/daughter a career or anything. Also the more you expect is the more you'll be let down and realise that it's not what you thought it would be.

Expect it to be a long hard journey from the start. At ages 5,6,7,8 and up managers may play their son/daughter in front of your child, going training 3-5 nights a week. The best thing I can say is to make things easy on yourself fnd a club that's close to you so it's not hard to get to training or matches. Get your child to play in a team that has a lot of their friends in it, don't be pressured into making decisions that you aren't 95-100% sure about.

Form your child don't expect much at a young age, don't think that they should be at a certain level by the time they're 6,7,8 or 9 and if theren't then they won't make it as a professional. On the other end of that spectrum if they're good and do have ability that is beyond their years, don't think this means that their also going to make it and start looking at them like a pension, that will get you out of the area you live in, buy you a big house or new car. Lots can and will happen before your child gets anywhere near being a professional footballer.

## A HEALTH MODE OF CONDUCT

The emotion roller-coaster that is football will find its way into your house at some point whether its from winning and losing games or from being a teenager and letting lose. You'll need to be as calm and balanced as you possibly can, to some this will be harder than for others. But losing your head and shouting at other parents of other children isn't the way forward. This will just make matters worse by making others around you feel scared and not wanting to bring their children. To you getting banned from attending matches, training etc. If another parent gets angry as well a fight could break out frightening everyone including your own child.

Encouraging your child from the sidelines is all part of the game but don't get confused with encouragement and dictation. When you dictate to your child what to do it only confuses them, how?. Imagine this; your child has an idea of what they want to do when they get on the pitch, then the manager tells them what they want them to do, then you add to this by shouting at them what to do from the sidelines. Now your child has 3 things going on in their head and they want to please everyone this is all too much for them to cope with. Even professional footballers don't have this problem, they only have their own idea and what the manager wants from them, the crowd is there encouraging them on by singing songs and cheering them on from the stands or trying to put them off in the same way. So don't do this to your child, especially when they're on trial at a new club where they're trying to fit in and show the best that they can be.

Encourage, be humble and respectful to the best of your ability, football is meant to be exciting, a place of dreams, somewhere you can get away from the realities of school, collage or work.

By having this health mode of conduct you and your child/children will enjoy football, giving them more chance to express themselves and excel.

*"Most children especially my son thrives and plays better from being encouraged and allowed to play his game without too much criticism from myself or his dad. Football for kids should first and foremost be fun.*
*Lastly, always wear layers! Even what looks like a sunny day can feel freezing on an open playing field and can turn at any time"*

**Angela Saunders. Mother to a youth academy footballer**

# PROFESSIONAL FOOTBALL ASSOCIATION (PFA)

The PFA is the oldest established sportsperson's union in the world, having been in continuous existence since 1907. The PFA helps their members throughout their footballing careers as well as the transition from the game.

I have worked with the PFA as a member before and interviewed staff members for this book.

Here are the interviews that conducted.

## Terry Angus

### 1. WHAT'S YOUR ROLE IN THE PFA?
Equalities Executive in Communities.

### 2. WHAT ADVICE CAN YOU GIVE YOUNGSTERS WANTING TO BECOME FOOTBALLERS?
Work hard at your training not just in sessions organised by coaches but also on your own. Be better at your good points and be good at your weaker areas. Also do not forget about your educational academic studies, these are vital as a different option.

### 3. WHAT ADVICE CAN YOU GIVE TEENAGERS PLAYING SEMI PRO OR ACADEMY FOOTBALL?
As in life you have to show resilience and character, running away is not always the answer. Speak to the coaches find out what areas you need to improve and work on those areas. Going out on loan can be beneficial, usually though if you are not getting sufficient game time however, this can have a negative effect. If released spend time to assess all options, speak to family friends and the PFA, also be pre-pared to drop down levels and/or return to education, training or employment.

## 4. YOUR TOP TIPS?

Work hard: Have options: Success comes in many formats: Recognise when you can now longer chase the dream by being honest with yourself: Don't try to live up to the perception of the footballer... Just be a footballer.


## George Bowyer

## 1. WHAT IS YOUR ROLE IN THE PFA?

My role is the PFA Independent Registration Service Advisor. The service offers free Independent advice on the EPPP and Youth Development Rules and Regulations, offering assistance to Academy Players, Parents, Carers and Guardians throughout a player's journey in the Academy system.


## 2.WHAT DO YOU THINK WOULD HELP YOUNGSTERS WHO WANT TO BECOME PROFESSIONALS TODAY?

Aspiring youngsters need to want to develop and learn to become the best that they can at every opportunity. As the development of training facilities and coaches continues to grow at every level, players now have a greater platform to help them reach their goals of playing at the highest level they can reach.


## 3.HOW CAN PARENTS HELP THEIR CHILDREN?

Parents and Guardians play an important role during a player's time in the Academy system, offering support and constructive feedback away from the Academy is important. Parents should be aware that all players will be faced with certain obstacles and challenges throughout their time and that it is not abnormal to go through highs and lows within this often competitive environment..

## 4. YOUR THREE TOP TIPS FOR WANNA BE FOOTBALLERS?

Listen, learn, and practice.

## 5. WHAT IS THE PFA SAFETY NET?

Making players and parents aware of the further support that is readily available to them at the time of entering or leaving the Academy system. The PFA Safety Net is an online platform which players and parents can access 24/7 by simply visiting www.thepfa-safetynet.com inputting their own details they can create their very own confidential support page.

Interview with Matthew Buck

Interview with George Bowyer

# AGENTS

83

The high profile footballer has to deal with many different aspects from the modern game, from chairmen to managers, players to fans, and sponsors to endorsers. Which is enough to deal with before dealing with the main issue their football. This is where an agent comes in. Hate em or love em at the highest level football agents are a fundamental part of the modern game, and at some point are the most influential people in what is a huge and complex mutlimillion pound business.

An agent is now a must for every top level footballer. What an agent does is look after almost all a players back end life. But 1st get them contracts at clubs, moving players from club to club, renegotiatiing existing contracts, getting players on loan to helping there general up keep off the pitch like there fiancees, ie helping a player buy a house, a car, to insurance on these things.

The first thing to remember and think about when you are looking for a agent (or if you already have an agent) is that, it's their job and in their job they work on a commission bases so the more they get for you is the more they get for themselves. Remember these agents have been working in football before you came along and they will be working when you leave, so you are a passing phase in their life's but at that time you are the most important thing in that phase.

A player can be signed to an agent legally at the age of 16 in the UK but it has been known that agents and clubs have taken young players on around the age of 13 and got them to sign pre-contracts by building relationships with the parents so as to get them to persuade there son to sign to the club or agent when they reach the age of 16, some clubs and agents even buy the parents cars or giving them money to keep them happy and the bond strong between them. This is where it can all get a bit out of hand as the parents who have the biggest influence on what happens to their child can make decisions based on what is happening in their lives at the moment, i.e. they could be struggling with money and sign a deal because it helps them financially instantly. But this could have the potential to mess things up in the long run. It would be advisable at this point take time to think about what is being offered and not to sign anything that hasn't been looked over by a third party

Someone who has no emotional connection to the situation. If the person also knows about contracts this would be a bonus but is not a necessity.

Football off the pitch is a business and the business can chew you up and spit you out before you've even kicked a ball. So you need to get educated on all the things that can happen within contracts or get someone who is educated on your side, like an agent.

To be an agent in the UK you needed to take a multiple choice exam with the Football Association (FA) some questions based around domestic and European law and not just football its self. The exam is quiet hard and there is not a high pass rate, after that if you pass you will be a legal football agent. Once you've passed you will answer to the powers that be, which are the FA and FIFA, the governing bodies of football.

The FA have nowmade a new position called FA Intermediary which is an online form you fill in and pay a yearly subscription. This position is the modern day agent, checkout the FA website to find out more if this job is of interest to you.

## AGENTS FEES AND TRANSFERRING OF PLAYERS

Transferring of players are made generally in this way, two clubs agree on the price of a player, the player and new club agree on wages, bonuses etc the paperwork is sent to the FA saying that they look after player X. The new percentages of money on the contract all tally up with the forms that the FA gives the agents. It then gets stamped and approved by the FA and the club then pays the FA and the FA pays the agent.

Agent's fees are usual 5-7% of the players guaranteed wages over the term of the contract. This is not set in stone, as there is ways that the agent may take a smaller amount of money up-front rather then receive the money over the period of the players contract. I.e. if a agents percent is £10,000 over 3 years they might say to the club give us £7000 up-front rather than £3,333 over the 3 years. When there is a lot of money being transferred around then the ugly head of corruption isn't far behind. This is where you can get rouge deals and underhand payments to look after you and family members.

Agents deal with a lot of things for footballers but not everything, there are things that the player may speak to the agent about which the agent doesn't have to help with. Depending on a player's relationship with their agent or agency and how big the issue is will depend on whether the agent may help or not. For example arranging baby sitters, dropping other family members around the place like a personal assistant isn't in an agents job, but they may do it depending on your relationship.

If players and agents want to part ways this can be done by mutual consent, a player can't just drop an agent and an agent can't just drop a player (apart from gross misconduct, negligence or contracts not being renewed) this has to been done together otherwise a court case will be imminent with one side feeling betrayed by the other. This is not a good thing for a player as they have to stay as focused as possible for football.
With all this in mind you have to always go back to the notion that it is your career, life and ultimately you have the final say in how it goes.
All decisions come down to you in other words. But don't to rational as i said before you are an asset and agents don't like losing assets, as that is money walking out the door, they will do the best they can for you to try and keep you.

## IS AN AGENT RIGHT FOR ME?

Agents can open doors for you to a whole world of new and fun adventures that you would have only dreamed about as a young boy, some of which will be exactly what you are looking for and some won't. They can also close these doors, again some of which you'll want them to and some you won't.
The best agent for you is the one that you think you'll be with for the whole duration of your life as a footballer. Because ultimately what you will be having with them is a relationship, and with all relationships trust is a major factor. If you feel you can trust them then you won't be looking over your shoulder or questioning things that they do, you'll know that your agent has got your back.
An agents working world and what they do for you is business and business isn't always laughs and smiles it can be very dark secretive place with many disap-

pointments. You'll have to learn to make decisions together as quickly as possible and move on to the next one, otherwise the more you think about them the harder they'll become.

To know if an agent is going to be right for you or not, i'd suggest looking on the internet at a few website and arrange to meet with a few and see what they can offer you and what vibe you get from them when you go from there.

Only look to do this is your of age 16 and up, and playing at academy, development centre, school of excellence or semi-pro team. Because lots of people contact top agents and they will all ask them these questions like, who do you play for? because they don't want to be wasting their time on a player that may not have the potential to make it into the professional game.

Interview with Aaron Maines

# FREESTYLE
# FOOTBALL

# FREESTYLE FOOTBALL

Freestyle football is quickly becoming one of the worlds fastest growing sports with 154 million people watching One Live World Championship Tfvour, run by The Freestyle Football Federation one of the sports world governing bodies in 2014. It will only be a matter of time before it becomes a mainstream sporting event not only watched on the internet but on tv channels.

Freestyle football is a way of juggling a ball in the air doing tricks in as many different ways as possible, showing artistic skills and an effortless smooth finesse in the way you do it. Because of this it's one of the easiest sports to do as you don't need other people or a big space or any fancy kit just you a ball and your mind to think of new exciting tricks and a sequence to put them in.

There are currently well over 1000 professional athletes making a full time living from doing freestyle football and the Football Freestyle Federation is established to significantly grow in the coming years through event structures and general popularisation of the sport.

A great thing about freestyle football is that you can be any age and you can have a longer career than if you become a professional footballer. I spoke to one of the sports governing bodies about the freestyle football world. Here is a few Q&A's from the interview which will help if you want to get into the freestyling world.

## 1, WHAT IS YOUR COMPANY CALLED?
The Freestyle Football Federation. Its world governing body for the sport of freestyle football.

## 2, WHAT OTHER COUNTRIES DO YOU WORK IN?
We work across 102 countries worldwide, promoting the sport and simple notion that 'all you need is a ball' to get active and enjoy this exciting sport.

## 3, HOW CAN YOU GET INTO FREESTYLING?
There is so much content out online for free so the best recommendation is to use our new platform www.freestylelife.tv which pulls together all the best content from around YouTube to one destination. This includes tutorial videos and much more from the best athletes. After this spark of inspiration you need to find a ball

90

and give it a go. It takes a lot of practice and resilience so you need to be prepared to fail in order to progress in this sport.

## 4, WHO DO YOU WORK WITH? ADVERTISING COMPANIES AND AGENTS?

We don't have any formal partners in the marketing or PR world. We have grown very organically and continue to seek partners in any sector to help us grow awareness and ultimately participation in the sport. Our ambassador is Ronaldinho from Brazil, which is certainly one name that gets the media attention.

## 5, HOW DO YOU MAKE MONEY IN FREESTYLING?

There are two sides to succeeding in freestyle. After mastering the ball and creating your own style, you could choose either (or both) of the following channels:

The Art:

To make money here you need to create short entertaining sequences of moves that are choreographed to music and perform this in the streets or at live events where brands will pay for this entertainment. You need to be active on social media and promote yourself regularly in many different ways in order to be in the public eye and therefore then get requests to perform.

The Sport:

Ideally you would also be able to participate in competitions that are staged by the Federation and our network also. There are different gradings of event from National to Continental and World Open status. Many of which offer prize money to the top 3 placings, but also these events give you an opportunity to be seen and sponsored also.

Either way it is a journey and should not be expected that money will just come flooding to you when you have a few skills. Patience, practice and resilience is key to success.

## 6, HOW DO PEOPLE GET IN TOUCH/FIND OUT MORE?

All information about the Federation and the sport can be seen at www.freestyle-football.org and enquiries can be sent to info@freestylefootball.org any time.

91

## 7, CAN ANYONE CONTACT YOU ABOUT ANY TIPS OR AD-VICE?

Yes, we welcome all enquiries at any time.

## 8, WHAT ADVICE WOULD YOU GIVE PEOPLE WANTING TO GET INTO THE FREESTYLING?

Do it! You don't need teachers, team mates or facilities. All you need is a ball! It is a fantastic lifestyle and community that will build your character, confidence and core fundamental skills.

## DANIEL WOOD

President • Freestyle Football Federation

Interview with Daniel Wood

92

# HEALTH & FITNESS

# HEALTH AND FITNESS

Your health and fitness are major factors to not only being able to play the game how you in-vision yourself playing, but also the key to playing the game at your highest level for as long as possible well into your 30s. In this chapter you'll find ways in which to do this and more. Improving your footballing and personal life.

## HEALTH

This is how you feel inside not only your inner body, muscles, lungs, heart etc but also your state of mind. The state of mind can be easily over looked in football, not just by players but also by all involved. Your mental state is just as important as your physical state or if not even more important. You can be in the best shape of your life but when your mind is not right, unfocused or confused by any issues on or off the field then your football will suffer. The great thing is that your mind works both ways, because if your mental state is great and you can't feel any better then you'll feel as if you can take on the world or can't lose anything and will take on all challenges confidently creating a winning ora about you.

## FITNESS

This is the bodies' physical state and how it copes with physical activity, and how it recovers/repairs itself. Your fitness is very very important in this day and age of football because of the way football has changed over the years. In general we are all becoming more aware of our bodies and our fitness, more and more people are doing exercises to look after their bodies. Just as important to your fitness training is what you eat and drink. You may be training as hard as you can but without supplying the body with the right nutriments, proteins and water etc then the body will not be able to; firstly perform correctly and secondly it won't be able recover properly.

94

Leaving you open to loads of muscles injuries also prolonging the road to recover from injuries. If you do eat and drink correctly then you will be able to perform how you want and recover properly enabling you to perform again and again increasing your levels of fitness.

## PREPARING YOURSELF FOR GAMES AND TRAINING.

In sport your mental state is constantly being challenged because of how great you feel when you win, and how bad you feel when you lose. Sometimes there is a thin line between winning and losing which will stay on your mind and play on it until you can put it to rest and move on. For some people freeing the mind of this is easier than for others. There are ways to help you control your mind and help you deal with this and other things.
So how do I get a healthy body and mind you may well be asking?.Here are a few suggestions.

## 1. RELAX.

Whatever takes you away from the daily pressures, start applying this to your day for at least 15-20 mins a day, if you can do it for more than do so. If you don't know what makes you relaxed then try something new like yoga, pilates, walking, reading, listening to music something to reduce the heart rate and give your mind and body time away from the hard pressures you ask of it daily. But this shouldn't include SLEEPING in the middle of the day. If you do this then you are training your body to fall asleep and get tired when really you need your body to be at its physical peak especially at around 3pm, when most of your games will be played at that time (If you're doing this stop now!).
Once you know how to relax yourself then this will help you to think more clearly and also help you assess situations in a clearer light.

## 2. EATING AND DRINKING PROPERLY.

You may have heard of the phrase you are what you eat. This is true in the context of what goes in to our bodies will determine how our bodies work, rest and recover. The human body is an amazingly orchestrated complex work of art made up from lots of proteins and complex chemicals. When we put into it outside chemicals (food and drink) that don't help the body when it uses lots of energy or what the body needs to help it repair itself (things like alcohol and large amounts of junk food) then the body is affected in many different ways. Muscles won't work or repair properly, they can pull and tear easier, get weaker over time, bones become weaker over time and can break easier. Also taking a much longer time to heal then they normally would. Joints can become stiff and ache making you less flexible and weaker, the brain will find it harder to send signals to the body. All of these effects will happen to you over a period of time which can be long or short depending on what and how much you put into your body. Alcohol and drugs are in a league of their own and to me are a no if you want to be a footballer.

## 3. GETTING THE RIGHT AMOUNT OF SLEEP.

You need sleep to help the body recover from all the activities and stress you have put on it during the day, so it can recharge and be ready for you to use the next day, and as a teenager to help produce your HGH. (human growth hormone) Many tests and surveys have been done about how much sleep an athlete should get, and 95% of them come back with the same results, that athletes should get around 9-10 hours sleep per day to perform well. One of these tests done in America saw tennis athletes who slept the 9-10 hours hit more accurate shots and ran faster sprints than the athletes who had 7-8 hours sleep.

In practice this all sounds easy but in reality this can be very hard for must people to achieve, because if you wanted to get up at 7am then you would need to be asleep by 9pm, and if you wanted to get up at 8am then you'd need to be asleep at 10pm etc etc. If you are a professional sportsmen or athlete then you shouldn't really have any excuses because this is your job and is something that can help you achieve greater success. But if you have to work or go to college and fit this in then it's a little harder, but still no excuse because where there's a will there is a way. Going to bed late is something that you shouldn't do as an athlete in training especially after being up all day either working or training as your body starts to slow down conserve energy and concentrates on repairing its-self getting ready for the next day. If you stay up really late then your messing around this recover period and setting yourself up for a harder day tomorrow.

## A LITTLE EXTRA.

If your semi professional or have a job or at college and looking to get into the professional game then you may not be getting all the exercise you need to, to be as fit as you need to be in the professional game. So you will have to find away in which you can get more training. Because if you want to be a professional then you have to train as much as they do so your as fit as they are or fitter leaving your footballing ability and knowledge as a player the onlt thing you need to improve.

For all involved in sport at any level you can always do more, if your training and playing hard then you may need to learn how to rest a little bit more. If your not playing or training hard then you need to start by doing one of them and then do the other. If your doing it all right playing, training, and resting well then you can educate yourself more, learning how to play the game better. Improving your knowledge of the game.
Football like all team sports is made up of people playing different positions working together. Each position requires a different skill set, which includes different knowledge, techniques and physical attributes so learn all about your position fast. If your a winger learn different ways to cross the ball from beating someone down the line to whipping it in from 30 yards out, when and where to cross, joining in with play and heading for example. Improve on the fitness needed to play your position i.e forwrads being able to have that quick burst of speed to get away from defenders. This will set you apart from the others in your position making you the best player for that position and very dangerous.

All of this is easier said then done so here is a little something for you to remember, and this goes for whatever you do in your life. Whatever you put in is what you'll get out. If you put in 50% of your time, energy and mental strength into something then you'll get back a 50% reward. If you put in 100% then you'll get a 100% reward and the best thing is, this is all up to you and no one else, so if you want big rewards then put in big efforts.

## WHAT IT TAKES TO SUCCEED

This is the part of the book that will set you apart from the rest, the part of the book that will show you where you stand and why, because this is about succeding and hardwork. (read and think where do you stand)
As a teenager while others will want to play computer games you'll want to practices football skills. While others are out playing with friends you will want to practices football drills having the dedication, determination and sacrifice you need to succeed in your quest to becoming a footballer.
Yes a level of talent is also needed but just that alone won't help you reach your goal. All great sports atheltes, Cristiano Ronaldo, Muhammad Ali, Michael Jordan, Usain Bolt and Serena Williams had a naturally ability to play their sport, but they also was/are some of the most hardest working. Ariving at training first and leaving the training field last, practicing new techniques to become better and better each year or to reinvent the way they had to play the older they got, still taking on all the new comers to their crowns.

This kind of dedication is what it takes, testing yourself all the time learning and creating new skills becoming the new Ronaldo or Jordan.
The road to success will be a long one with lots of failures, but don't be put off by all the disappointments most of this will happen in the beginning when you are learning something new which is to be expecte,  but once this has passed and you have mastered it then success will be the only outcome.
So practice fail and practice again until you practice and succeed.

# BRAIN TRAINING

A footballers brain has to receive information, process it and make a decision on what to do very quickly, sometimes in a split second. The average footballer can do this quickly, but the top footballers can do this even quicker sometimes as if they know what going to happen before it does as if they can read the minds of their opponents. If you can add this ability which is to anticipate what your opponent is going to do next then you'll be one steps ahead of them.

This may seem very hard to achieve, but when you think about what it is there doing then it becomes easier to understand and more achievable for you to do.

SO HERE GOES:
What they're doing is accessing the cerebrum or cortex. The cerebral cortex is divided into four sections, called "lobes": the frontal lobe, parietal lobe, occipital lobe, and temporal lobe. The frontal lobe- associated with reasoning, planning, parts of speech, movement, emotions, and problem solving. Parietal lobe- associated with movement, orientation, recognition, perception of stimuli. Occipital lobe- associated with visual processing. Temporal lobe- associated with perception and recognition of auditory stimuli, memory, and speech. So you need to develop this part of the brain to perform these tasks quicker and better in much the same way that we train our bodies to run faster, be stronger and generally be fitter. There are many exercises that can help you to do this. Here are a few, much like the body the brain develops at different stages in our lives, so the programme has been written for different ages.

5-12 years old:
At this age your young brain will be absorbing a lot of information to do with life skills, so developing it for sport is something that you don't need to do. What you should be doing is enhancing these life skills lessons or so called motor skills to help with your sport. Lessons like balancing, co-ordination, hand and eye co-ordination. Doing kick ups is the best exercise to caputre all of these, also learning

## 99

basic football drills like going in and out of cones placed in a stright line and playing as many matches as you can.

13 - 19 years old:
This is the most crucial of times to do brain training because you will have a lot of other aspects to deal with that will play a major part in your development and life. Like puberty and hormones as well as being very experimental trying out lots of new things. So not only training the brain but dealing with emotions will be key here. Drinking and other harmful influences will slow down and affect the development of the brain so i'd advice not to take any of these substances.
At this age you'll need to learn self control and how to be focused, games that make you learn how to concentrate longer are good. Qiucker reaction games are good like batak. Learning to do 2 things at a time eg, reciving the ball and thinking what to do next, juggling, playing an instrument, balancing while catching a ball etc.

20 years old and up:
At this stage you'll be peaking physically and mentally, the things you'll need to be doing here is adapting your mind to match your body. So learn how to play the game according to your body eg, if your not qiuck learn how to get space and time on the picth so you don't need to be quick. Puzzle solving games and non-verbal reasoning exercises are good too practice.

By training your body and brain you will be becoming more of a complete player and someone that will be able to perform at 95-100% of their capabilities. Look at it this way, a perfect body and a wayward mind you'll perform at 80% of your capabilites.
A perfect mind and a unfit body you'll perform at 70% of your capabilites. A perfect body and perfect mind you'll perform at100% of your capabilites.
This will also give you a better life off the pitch, as you'll be more in tune with what you trying to achieve on the pitch and will be able to know what it will take off the pitch to help you on it.

There are many different brain training exercises on the internet the best ones for football are the ones that involve reactions like pressing buttons at the same time as reading whats on the screen, ones that make you do two things at once. Something physical and mental.

## HELPING YOU TO CONTROL YOU NERVES.

Calming the nerves is important in all sports because what you are doing is learning to control the signals that are being sent to the muscles and body by the brain and the nervous system. Sometimes even before a game a player can become so nerves that they make themselves sick or have nose bleeds because their body is running on overdrive, this doesn't happen to everybody but we all have a little nerves before going out to play in an important game or performing in front of big crowds and on trials.
So how can we control this?

### 1. Be confident in your abilities and what you can do.
This is something you can do by yourself by practicing, practicing, practicing and trying to perfect more and more different parts of your game and most of all perfecting the basics.

### 2. Knowing what your up against and how to combat it.
By doing research on your opponent and finding out their weaknesses and use them to your advantage. Have a game paln.

### 3.Relaxing yourself.
Do whatever it takes to relax yourself and bring down your heart rate. Most people listen to music, the Brazilian team like to play instruments almost like having a calypso party before a game.

# DRILLS, SKILLS & TECHNIQUES

# LEARNING THE TECHNIQUES

These drills will help you in your game and development, the most important thing is to practice but making sure you do the drills as best as you can improving each time, not just doing them half hearted as this will not improve your technique but waste your time. Also while your learning these new skills once you've mastered a few you can add your own skills to them, developing them even more putting your own flavour on them, making you become even more individual and unique. Football is about enjoyment, inspiration, creation showing people things that they wish they could do and enjoy watching, both young and old.

You learn things at different ages because of the physical and mental way your body develops over the years. The drills are age apropreate.

From about 6-11 years old:
Balancing and co-ordination drills.
• Ball Control: passing, dribbling, controlling, etc.
• Basic Skill: heading, shooting, step overs, etc.
• Basic Understanding of the game: throw-ins, defending, attacking
(off -sides at 11 years old)
• The drills should be fun for teams and individuals

12 -17 years old:
All the above plus,
• Ball Skills higher learning
• Balancing Leading to Strengthening
• Fitness
• Ball Controlling higher learning
• Understanding the Game: tactics, positioning, reading of the game, etc

18 years and up

All the above plus,

• Higher learning of the game: triangler play, reading of the game • Controlling emotions.

• Perfecting ball control

• Speeding up your thought process and play of football.

## HERE ARE A FEW DRILLS, SKILLS AND TECHNIQUES FOR YOU TO LEARN.

Simply scan the qr codes.

(the qr reader i used is 'qr reader by TapMedia Ltd) for constant updates and new drills, skills and techniques to learn subscribe to my Dean Holness Youtube channel or Dean Holness Vimeo channel.

Here is an interview about strength and conditioning with Brain Walpole who has worked with many different professional clubs over many years including the German World Cup winning side of 2014.

### Interview with Brian Walpole

*"Remember good training will produce good results, great training will produce great results & bad training will produce bad results, Quality is better than Quantity"*

## Dean Holness Southend United

Brian Walpole
Strength Training

Brian Walpole
Speed Training

The Double Step Over

Dribbling Practice

The Samba Flip Flap

The Twistcat

107

The Step Over                     Skill Dubs

The Cruyff Turn

Flick Over Head

Speed Training Ball Work

The 360 & Double 360

# A 12 WEEK PROGRAMME TO IMPROVE YOUR FOOTBALL ABILITY.

To use this programme properly use the drills from my Dean Holness Youtube channel and mix them with drills from your teams training and your own ideas. Visit my website to download your free 12 week programme, which is also age appropriate. www.deanholness.co.uk

| | | | | | | | |
|---|---|---|---|---|---|---|---|
| Week 1 | Basic Footwork | Ball control | Kick up Practice | Dribbling | | Basic Passing | Match Day |
| Week 2 | Free Session | Basic Control | Passing | Fun Skills | | Dribbling | Match Day |
| Week 3 | Basic Footwork | Passing | Kick up Practice | Dribbling | | Basic Control | Match Day |
| Week 4 | Free Session | Ball Control | Passing | Fun Skills | | Dribbling | Match Day |
| Week 5 | Basic Footwork | Dribbling | Kick up Practice | Control | | Basic Passing | Match Day |
| Week 6 | Free Session | Basic Control | Passing | Fun Skills | | Dribbling | Match Day |
| Week 7 | Basic Footwork | Intermediate control | Kick up Practice | Dribbling | | Passing | Match Day |
| Week 8 | Free Session | Basic Control | Hard | Fun Skills | | Dribbling | Match Day |
| Week 9 | Basic Footwork | Intermediate passing | Kick up Practice | Dribbling | | Intermediate Control | Match Day |
| Week 10 | Free Session | Intermeiate Control | Hard Passing | Fun Skills | | Dribbling | Match Day |
| Week 11 | Basic Footwork | Dribbling | Kick up Practice | Intermediate Control | | Hard Passing | Match Day |
| Week 12 | Free Session | Intermediate Control | Hard Passing | Fun Skills | | Dribbling | Match Day |

# NUTRITION

# WHAT IS NUTRITION

Nutrition is the process of providing or obtaining the food necessary for health and growth within the body and brain. Sports nutrition as we now know is just as important as the physical exercise and training itself. It helps you to train harder, be stronger, recovery quicker and maintain a healthy body.

Not only does eating and drinking the right food help the body it also helps the brain, as certain nutrients from the food you eat can develop the brain especially when you are young. On the flip side of this, if you eat and drink things that harm the body and brain then these effects can happen to you poor muscle and bone growth, eg heavy alcohol consumption can prevent good brain development.

So its very important to know what to put into the body and the right amounts. Knowing what is good nutrition and bad nutrition is simple when it comes to things like alcohol, sweets, chocolates and fast foods but its the area of proteins, carbohydrates and fats where people get confused and don't know what is right and wrong. It isn't made any easier when the internet is full of people obsessed by diets and weight loss all claiming they know the quickest way to do it, with many different programmes and fitness channels showing you their way but never fully explaining how it works or the real benefits/side affects from what your doing.

We are all different and foods will reacted differently to each individual.

I interviewed sports nutritionist Matt Lovell who has been England international rugby teams nutritionist for 15 years, Tottenham Hotspurs nutritionist for 6 years, Manchester Citys nutritionist for 6 years and also Millwalls when they reached the reached the FA cup final in 2004.

Matt gave me a breakdown of what he tells his athletes to eat for them to play at the highest level possible. We also spoke about the right nutrition for kids and teenagers with match day meals, recovery meals, protein shakes etc. With these guidelines you'll be able to not only to prepare your body for football, but also understand what it is you are doing and why.

## 112

Interview with Matt Lovell

# 1. WHAT BASIC FOOD KNOWLEDGE DO WE NEED TO KNOW TO HELP WITH PHYSICAL TRAINING AND DEVELOPMENT?

Nutrition for young adult footballers.

Eating for energy.

Your plates of food should look something like the one below, in order to consume enough energy for a sporting lifestyle, and to provide the nutrients needed for good health.

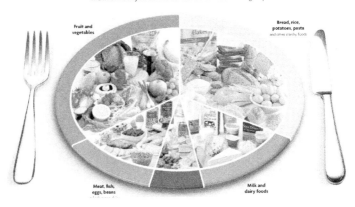

## The eatwell plate

Use the eatwell plate to help you get the balance right. It shows how much of what you eat should come from each food group.

Fruit and vegetables

Bread, rice, potatoes, pasta and other starchy foods

Meat, fish, eggs, beans

Milk and dairy foods

Each meal should consist of a portion of protein, complex carbohydrate and vegetables. Carbohydrate should be the major source of energy. Eating plenty of carbohydrate from fruit and vegetables, which are high in fibre, vitamins and minerals, helps to allow this energy to be released slowly to maintain a steady supply of energy.

Carbohydrate
• Carbohydrate is the body's primary energy source, essential for intense exercise. It is stored in a readily used form called glycogen in the muscles.
• You need to ensure an adequate supply for training and competition, and be sure to replenish levels afterwards.
• Throughout the day, whole grains should be eaten to provide a constant supply of energy.

Good Carbohydrate Choices:
• Whole-grain and Sesame-seed bagels
• Rye Bread
• Whole-wheat bread
• Whole-wheat pita bread
• High fibre cereals (shredded wheat, all bran, branflakes)
• Quinoa
• Couscous
• Whole-wheat crackers
• Pasta
• Rice (preferably brown or wild)
• Whole-wheat pretzels
• Beans and peas (garbanzo, pinto, kidney, white split, lima, black-eyed)
• Lentils
• Fruitful fruits:
• Pineapple, Apricots, Kiwis, Black-cherries, Mango, Pears, Bananas (pre-training especially)

## Protein

• Protein is the main structural component of muscle tissue and provides building blocks for structures in your cells –about 15% of your daily energy intake should come from protein.

• Protein should be included at every meal, this will help control blood glucose levels support muscle and improve appetite regulation.

• Choose lean meat and poultry, avoiding prepared meals and processed meats (Preparation!). Fish is a superb source of protein, it is low in saturated fat and oily fish like mackerel are also high in omega-3 fatty acids.

• Peas and beans (legumes) are excellent vegetarian sources of protein, carbohydrate and fibre. Most plant proteins do not contain all the essential amino acids (animal protein does);.

• Nuts are also a useful protein source but they should be eaten in moderation as they have a high fat content.

116

# Fat

• Not all fats are bad. Our body needs fat to give us energy, to construct our muscles, nerves, hormones and insulate our bodies for warmth. Cutting out fats from your diet would mean you would be cutting a large chunk out of the eat- well plate; for example, fats help us absorb certain vital vitamins.

• Unsaturated fats (poly unsaturated & mono-unsaturates) are often called "good fats" and include important fatty acids such as omega 3. These are important building blocks for our brain cells and hormones.

• Saturated fats should be kept to a lower intake and eaten in moderation.

"Good Fat" Foods:
• Oily fish
◻ Mackerel
◻ Kippers
◻ Salmon
◻ Trout
• Flaxseeds
• Walnuts
• Pumpkin seeds
• Hazelnuts
• Almonds
• avocados,
• olives,

## 2. WHAT ABOUT WATER CONSUMPTION?

The concept of good hydration is a simple one; if you sweat more you need to drink more. It is however something that is regularly misjudged by athletes even those playing at the top level. Thirst tends to come on late and be satisfied early so your own body cues aren't always enough to go on.

Optimal Hydration is essential to maximise performance and preserve health. Losing just 2% of your body weight through sweat will negatively affect both mental and physical performance.

Fluid losses in sport are often accompanied by high electrolyte (salt) losses, including excretion of sodium, potassium, calcium, magnesium and chloride. These may seriously impact on concentration, strength, exercise performance and endurance. Practical advice: "What do I do?"

## • MONITORING URINE VOLUME OUTPUT AND COLOUR

A large amount of light colour, diluted urine probably means you are hydrated; dark coloured, concentrated urine probably means you are dehydrated.

You can download a pee chart from on the internet to show you the colour of urine needed to be hydrated or dehydrated.

If possible put it near your toilet so you can monitor your urine, especially on a match day.

118

Football is a particularly "Hot Topic"
• Football and other "intermittent sports" (where you repeatedly sprint, then re-cover) are particularly prone to dehydration.
• Monitor urine colour and see how this relates to how you fell over the day.
• You should rehydrate with electrolyte solutions (salts) to replace 1.5xsweat- losses!
• Have a bottle with you at ALL TIMES – in school, training, at home – everywhere. Drink from a bottle of water to measure daily intake until you are used to drinking enough.

• Rehydration drinks contain salts, and it's also advisable to drink water when you eat food. If making your own, use full-sugar squash for recovery, or diluted fruit juice or low sugar-squash at other times, adding a pinch of salt.

Making a Sports Drink You will need...

• Full-sugar Cordial
• Low sugar Cordial
• Fruit juice
• Water
• Salt

When doing low intensity workouts.
Full-sugar cordial and water.
Low sugar cordial and water.
Great for before and during your match or training sessions.

When doing High intensity workouts.
Fruit juice and salt.
Great for during and after your match or training sessions.

## 3. FROM YOUTH TO TEENAGER TO ADULTHOOD YOUR BODY WILL GO THROUGH MANY CHANGES, HOW CAN WE HELP THIS PROCESS WITH NUTRITION ESPECIALLY IN SPORT?

As you're growing and active, you'll likely have higher demands for nutrients than a lot of adults.

The most important when considering eating as a growing athlete is energy – this is measured in calories. It Is vital you eat enough calories to keep growing, adapting, and improving after your training sessions.

These calories come from carbohydrate, fat, and protein. Each of these nutrients contains a certain amount of calories (kcal) per gram:

- 1g Carbohydrate = 4 kcal
- 1g Fat = 9 kcal
- 1g Protein = 4 kcal

Fat has the most calories per gram. If you eat too many foods that are high in fat you will consume more calories than you use, and are likely to gain weight.
you should eat a high carbohydrate diet, topped up with good fats. Take in protein around exercise!

The amount of calories you eat or drink depends on;

- Age,
- Gender,
- Training-load,
- Whether you are trying to lose, maintain or gain weight.

As a rough guide:

- Children (7-10 years old) should consume = 2000calories every day (when resting)
Add an extra 500Kcal for an easy training-day
- Adolescents (15-18 years old) should consume...
- Males: 3000 Kcal per day
- Females: 2200 Kcal per day

## 120

As an example, you need to be eating at least 3 moderately sized meals a day or 5-6 smaller ones. If you were to consume 3 moderate, carb-based meals as above, along with drinks and recovery snacks around training, this would constitute about 2000 Kcal.

The Golden Rules:
• It is vital you eat frequently – don't skip breakfast
. breakfast cereal, toast and yoghurt. Baked beans on whole-grain toast. Fruit salad with yogurt.
. Muesli with raisins.
• To consume enough calories look for high carb foods, with sources of good fats.


Examples:
Sardines on toast.
Peanut Butter and Banana Sandwich, Nuts and dried fruit.
A Young footballer should try to eat more...Oily fish
The essential fats within help build your brains, eyes and prevent symptoms of overtraining. If you can't stomach fish, these fats can be obtained from a variety of good quality, flavoured fish-oils. They DONT taste as bad and will help you function physically and mentally.

Milk for Calcium and Protein - Don't Ditch the Dairy!
Milk is already a great protein shake, containing protein and carbohydrate in an ideal ratio for recovering from exercise. They blend of slow release (casein) and fast release (whey) proteins supports training adaptation, helping us get ftter faster!

## 4. WHAT WOULD BE A GOOD MEAL PLAN FOR TRAINING OR MATCH DAYS, AND WHAT TIMES ARE BEST TO EAT TO GET THE MAXIMUM OUT OF YOUR FOOD?

Nutrition for intense training and competition should be focused on providing lots of good quality carbohydrate-rich foods. Match days may see this need increased, allowing you to take in more sugars and high energy foods than during regular training. The following high-carb ideas can be used for match days, and can be reduced slightly for normal training practices.

The day before the Match Starts.

Consume an abundance of (good, colourful, slow-release) carbs – reduce sugar and fats

## THE DAY OF THE MATCH:

## HIGH CARB BREAKFAST

• Eating a good breakfast will give enough time to start topping up your body's glycogen stores, which will help ease the burden on your muscles during exercise.

• If you do not have enough time, or find it hard to eat large quantities in the morning, at least try to eat some form of high-carb snack – many athletes find consuming bars, gels, drinks and convenient sports-foods can help.

• Breakfast Ideas:

. breakfast cereal, toast and yoghurt.

. Baked beans on whole-grain toast.

. Fruit salad with yogurt.

. Muesli with raisins.

Pre-match meal – 2-4 hours before, depending on your ability to handle food on game day.

. pasta/rice/noodles with protein e.g. stir fry noodles with lean beef strips.

. jacket potato with beans, tuna, or meat topping.

. Bread rolls with salad and protein filling e.g. chicken, egg, cheese, ham etc.

. Poached egg and/or beans on toast

• Although many studies have shown that physical performance is rarely impaired, some football players may be best avoiding sports drinks, gels and confectionary until closer to training as a "sugar crash" may hinder concentration.

If you suffer from pre-match nerves use meal replacements/drinks:

☒ Cereal bars e.g. Go-Ahead bar, Alpen, Special K, Nutrigrain.

☒ Fruit e.g. canned fruit, fresh fruit.

☒ White bread with honey or jam.

☒ Soft sweets e.g. jelly-cubes, jelly babies. Boiled sweets and liquorice are not suitable.

☒ Sports drink e.g. SiS Go or Lucozade Sport.

# MEAL PLANS FOR YOU QUICK AND EASY. MATCH-DAY

## BREAKFASTS

### SCOTCH PANCAKES — 10minutes

• Scotch pancakes – serves 2

• 100g Self raising  flour

• 2 Eggs – large

• 100ml milk (can use goat's, sheep's or Lactose-free pre-treated milk if intolerant)

• Coconut oil to grease the pan

Sift the flour, mix the ingredients and fry in small rounds, turning half way through. Serve with berries and yogurt. The more active your day, the more of the plate should be occupied by pancake – the easier your day, the more should be yogurt and fruit!

## PROTEIN PORRIDGE - 5 minutes
• 1 heaped "scoop" oats (50g) 1 scoop whey-protein (30g)

Boil the kettle and cover oats with water in a pan. Stir until thickened.

OR

Microwave and stir after every 10 sec.

Stir whey into hot porridge with lots of water. This will thicken it to a gloopy porridge-consistency!

## LIQUID BREAKFASTS – SPEEDY SMOOTHIES!
Put ingredients in a blender... then press "on"!!!

## APPLE STRUDEL
• Cold water or skimmed milk
• 1⁄2 can rice pudding
• 200ml milk
• 1⁄2 container (3.9 oz) natural unsweetened apple sauce
• Cinnamon as desired
• 1 tsp peanut butter
• 250mls of skim milk
• 1/2 cup of low fat or fat-free cottage cheese
• 2 tablespoons of natural peanut butter
• 1 tablespoon of linseeds, & 1⁄2 table spoon of lecithin granules

## STRAWBERRIES AND CREAM
• 200mls skimmed milk
• 1 small, low-fat, strawberry yogurt
• 2-3 Tbsp. of sugar-free rice pudding and or low fat condensed milk
• A handful of strawberries

# CARB-FUELLED LUNCHES AND DINNERS.

When making these quick, easy dinners, you can then pre-portion some packed lunches for later in the week. This saves time and money as you don't have to keep buying lunch. You can also ensure that what you eat is healthy – you're not at the mercy of the local chippy!

Many of these recipes can be assembled from jars, cans and packets if you're not too great in the kitchen. The complexity increases for the more adventurous amongst you, but keeping it simple can help save time.

## POSH BEANS ON TOAST
• 1 can mixed beans (cannellini, haricot, kidney etc)
• 1 tsp Paprika
• 1dsp tomato puree
• Sea salt and pepper
• 1tsp honey
• 2 slices granary toast
• (Can serve with a couple of poached eggs to increase protein)

## HEALTHY PIZZA
1 Pizza base (see below for recipe to make your own really healthy version!)
1 jar of rich tomato sauce with herbs and garlic – e.g. Dolmio, (or "Weight-Watchers" for low-fat)
• 1 Low-fat Mozzarella (e.g. Supermarket "Healthy" ranges)
• 1 can of Tuna
• 1/2 an onion (diced)
• Olives (in brine)
• Capers (in brine)
• 1/2 sliced Red Pepper

## PIZZA BASE:
• 250g strong wholemeal bread our or Tipo '00' our
• or 200g strong wholemeal bread our or Tipo '00' our, plus 200g finely ground semolina our (alternatively, use gluten free our or a more easily digestible form of wheat – spelt)
• 1/2 tsp sea salt
• 1/2 x 7g sachets of dried yeast
• 1/2 tsp golden caster sugar
• 1 tablespoon extra virgin olive oil
• 175ml lukewarm water

Sieve the flour/s and salt on to a clean work surface and make a well in the middle. Mix the yeast, sugar and olive oil into the water and leave for a few minutes, then pour into the well. Using a fork, bring the flour in gradually from the sides and swirl it into the liquid. Keep mixing, drawing larger amounts of flour in, and when it all starts to come together, work the rest of the flour in with your clean, flour-dusted hands. Knead.

Place the ball of dough in a large flour-dusted bowl and flour the top of it. Cover the bowl with a damp cloth and place in a warm room for about an hour until the dough has doubled in size.

Now remove the dough to a flour-dusted surface and knead it around a bit to push the air out with your hands – this is called knocking back the dough. You can either use it immediately, or keep it, wrapped in cling film, in the fridge (or freezer) until required.

## NEPTUNO PIZZA
Dough above makes 2 medium pizzas. Each serves 1 for a main
• Pre made tomato-sauce/passata to cover base
• Chopped garlic
• 1 small can (100g) preserved artichokes hearts
• 1 can albacore tuna
• King prawns
• Capers

## VEGETARIAN EGG AND ASPARAGUS

Dough above makes 2 medium pizzas. Each serves 1 for a main
Per Serving = 505 Kcal, 30g Pro, 65g CHO, 14g Fat (add an extra 45Kcal and 5g fat for a smearing of tapenade)

• Pre made tomato-sauce/passatta to cover base
• Chopped garlic
• Chopped onion
• 2 raw eggs – they will fry as pizza cooks
• Asparagus spears
• 1 tbs Olive Tapenade (optional)


## SWEET-POTATO AND CHICK-PEA CURRY

• Coconut oil
• 1 tsp garam masala
• 1 tsp cumin
• 1 "thumb" (sized piece) of ginger
• 1 small chili – seeds depending on preference
• 1-2 cloves garlic
• 1 Red onion
• 1 sweet potato – finely sliced
• 1 can chick peas
• 1/2 can coconut-water
• 1 tsp tomato puree
• Dried apricots
• Dried figs
• Fresh coriander
• rice – mix of half-and-half wild and white rice
• (Optional) Spinach. Ketchup!

127

How to cook:

Over a high heat, start cooking the sliced sweet potato in a pan greased with the minimum coconut oil (as in the instructions above).

Add the spices, garlic and ginger to the pan.

Add the onion and reduce the heat to gradually soften – keep it moving so it doesn't stick!

When the sweet potato has started to colour and the onion soften, add the chick-peas with a little water, along with the coconut water, tomato puree, and dried fruit. Finish with coriander – you can also add spinach and wilt this down. If you have trained hard (this is the ONLY time you should have simple sugars!), then you may want to add some ketchup.

You can then use leftovers to fill wraps/tupper-ware boxes for the week's lunch.

## CHICKEN & WHITE BEAN SALAD

Can you make a great meal from cans (with fresh veg)? YES!

Salad

1/4 can cannelloni or other white beans, rinsed and drained

1 diced cooked chicken breast

1 cup diced courgette

1/2 cup diced celery

1/4 cup finely diced feta cheese

1 dsp chopped sun-dried tomatoes (optional)

1 dsp coarsely chopped fresh basil, plus whole basil leaves for garnish 1/2 torn let-tuce

Vinaigrette

1 medium clove garlic

1/4 tsp salt

5 tablespoons extra-virgin olive oil

6 tablespoons fresh orange juice, plus more to taste

1/4 cup white-wine vinegar or red-wine vinegar

1 tablespoon Dijon mustard

How to cook:
Prepare vinaigrette. Combine beans, chicken, courgettes (and/or summer squash), celery, cheese and sun-dried tomatoes (if using) in a large bowl until well blended. Add chopped basil and vinaigrette; toss until combined. Taste and season with salt and/or pepper, if desired. Toss with romaine. Serve the salad garnished with fresh basil leaves.


## 5. WHAT'S YOUR ADVICE FOR RECOVERY FOODS AND DRINKS PRE, DURING, POST TRAINING AND MATCH DAYS?

Recovery – Post Training

Recovery is the ability of an athlete to perform quality work following a previous training session. The two most important factors in recovery are:

• Rest
• Nutrition

After training is when the muscles are most receptive to taking on nutrients in order to repair themselves and re-load energy stores. Therefore, adequate nutrition in recovery is the most effective way to fuel the next training session!

However, Carb fuelling and re-loading isn't the same as eating as much as you can!

Immediately after a heavy exercise session there is a "window of opportunity" to speed up recovery...
• Carbohydrate replenishment to fuel subsequent high-quality training sessions must begin immediately post training.
• Eating carbohydrate containing foods and fluids in the first hour or so after finishing the match will mean that your muscle glycogen stores are restocked more quickly and you are less likely to feel at the next.

• Having a little bit of protein at this time will also help to repair your muscle, improve glycogen storage and satisfy your appetite.

• If training twice a day then this may better consumed as a series of smaller servings, rather than a large meal, while it becomes increasingly important to provide quality sources of protein.

• High glycemic-index carbohydrates (SUGARY carbs, that are quickly digested) are the best choices AFTER INTENSE TRAINING as they provide the carbohydrate quickly that is more available for recovery

## RECOVERY MEALS WHEN YOU GET HOME

These meals provide the magic combination of protein and carbohydrates for recovery. The Carbs give your body energy to recover, whilst the protein gives your muscle the building blocks for growth and repair. They also contain enough good fats to supply you with energy and support good health.

## CHILLI CON CARNE
### Serves 2-4
• 2lb lean mince beef
• Olive oil
• 1 red onion
• 4-6 mushrooms
• 2 garlic cloves
• 1 red chilli 1 can of chopped tomatoes
• 1 can of red kidney beans
• Worcestershire sauce
• 1 small tub of soured cream

How to cook:

Chop garlic, onion, chilli and roughly chop the mushrooms. Heat 2-4 tablespoons of olive oil in frying pan - medium heat. Add all the chopped ingredients to the pan for 3-4 minutes when you should be hit with the garlic and chilli smells – fantastic. Turn the heat right up and add the mince. Season well and cook until brown in colour. Reduce the heat and add the tomatoes, 1 tablespoon of Worcestershire sauce and the kidney beans

## HEALTHY BURGERS

Makes 2 •burgers

300g premium very lean beef mince 1 egg white, lightly beaten

1/2 cup fresh breadcrumbs

1/2 teaspoon dried mixed herbs

1/2 teaspoon chilli powder

Freshly ground black pepper, to taste

How to cook:

Place the mince, egg, breadcrumbs and herbs into a bowl.

Add pepper to taste. Using your hands, mix until well combined, divide into two equal portions and shape each into a patty. Cook patties in a grill or lean grilling machine to minimise fat content. Serve with burger buns and salad

## COTTAGE PIE WITH CARROT AND SWEET POTATO MASH

Serves 4

• 500g extra-lean minced beef
• 1 clove garlic, peeled and crushed
• 1 large onion, peeled and chopped
• 2 carrots, washed, trimmed and diced
• 2tbsp plain  our
• 500ml beef stock
• 1tbsp Worcestershire sauce
• 1tbsp tomato puree
• salt and freshly ground black pepper

131

• For the mash:
• 500g sweet potato, peeled and cut into chunks
• 225g carrots, peeled and cut into chunks
• a knob of low-fat spread or butter
How to cook:
Heat a large non-stick frying pan and add the mince. Fry stirring ocasionally until browned. Add the garlic, onion and carrots and cook for a further 2mins. Stir in the our and cook for 1min. Add the stock to the pan, stirring, then add the Worcestershire sauce and tomato puree. Season with black pepper. Bring
to the boil and simmer for 10-15mins, removing the lid for the final 5 mins. Meanwhile, cook the potatoes and carrots in a large pan of lightly salted water for 15mins or until both are tender. Drain well then mash with the low-fat spread or butter. Season with black pepper. Cover and set to one side. Spoon the mince into a large shallow dish, then top with the carrot and potato mash, smoothing the surface. Place under a pre-heated grill for 4-5mins or until the top is golden brown. Serve hot with steamed vegetables.
You can also freeze this dish in a suitable container for up to 3 months. Thaw the dish thoroughly when you come to cooking and place in the oven at 200C/Fan 180C/Gas 6 for 25mins.

## CHICKEN AND PASTA SALAD
Serves 4
• 500g spiral pasta
• 2 cups frozen vegetables (peas, corn, diced carrot)
• 1 barbecued chicken
• 2 stalks celery, chopped 125g (1/2 cup)
• low-fat mayonnaise 125g (1/2 cup)
• low-fat natural yoghurt
• 1 tablespoon lemon juice
• 1 teaspoon finely grated lemon rind
• 2 teaspoons chopped fresh dill, (optional)
• freshly ground black pepper, to taste

## 132

How to cook:

Cook the pasta in a large pan of boiling water until al dente. Rinse under cold water and drain well. Cook the vegetables according to packet instructions. Remove the meat (minus skin and fat) from the chicken and chop it roughly. Combine the pasta, vegetables, chicken and celery in a large bowl. Mix the mayonnaise, yoghurt, lemon juice, rind and dill in a small bowl, then add to the pasta mixture. Toss to mix the dressing through the salad and season to taste

If you can't find barbeque chicken, just dice up 4 chicken breasts and add a dry packet barbeque spice mix (e.g. Schwartz) or sticky barbeque sauce to the chicken once cooked.

Serve with salad and bread rolls

## TUNA PASTA BAKE
### Serves 4-6

- 1 red, green and yellow pepper
- 375-500g penne pasta
- 1 tsp olive oil
- 1 tsp crushed garlic
- 1 small onion, thinly sliced
- 3 courgettes, sliced
- 1/2 cup balsamic vinegar
- 400g can tuna in brine, drained
- 150g low-fat cottage cheese
- 1 cup ultra-light sour cream (10% fat)
- 1/2 cup chopped fresh basil
- freshly ground black pepper

How to cook:

Place peppers, skin-side up, under grill and cook for 8-10 minutes or until charred and blistered.

Transfer to a heatproof bowl, cover with a plate or foil and set aside for 5 minutes (this helps to loosen the skin). Peel skin and slice flesh into strips. Pre-heat oven to 180OC (350 OF). Cook pasta according to packet instructions, drain. Meanwhile, spray a non-stick saucepan with oil and cook garlic onion over medium heat for

3 minutes or until soft. Add courgette and vinegar and cook for further 3-5 minutes or until soft. Combine pepper, pasta and courgette mixture with tuna, cottage cheese, sour cream, basil and pepper and transfer to an ovenproof dish or 4 individual dishes. Bake for 15 minutes or until golden brown.

## 5, BULKING UP & GETTING LEAN, WHAT AGE SHOULD YOU TAKE PROTEIN SHAKES & WEIGHT GAINING FOOD?

In order to stay strong on the ball, make tackles, and win contested balls in the air, football players require high levels of power and strength. Football is a contact-sport after all! Power is defined as the amount of force produced in a given time being strong quickly!. This requires the muscle to be efficient at producing force, and players require a certain base-level of strength in order to be powerful.

Some players may feel they would benefit from increasing muscle-mass in order to improve their strength, the quality of their weights-training, and their power- production on the pitch.

After training the body repairs and adapts during recovery in order to get fitter and stronger. Including the right types of nutrients during this recovery period can stimulate your body adapt in a specific way, helping your body improve following specific training sessions. Eating specifically for each session is never so important as when we are trying to increase muscle-mass. Eating the right types and quanti- ties of carbs and proteins, at the correct time rein relation to training, will stimulate the muscles to grow following resistance training.

Nutritional Requirements for Bulking Up: More than Just Protein, Protein Intake
• During periods of hypertrophy or reduced calorie intake athletes should consume approximately 1.7g/kg of body weight per day.

• This is easily obtainable even in a vegetarian diet that contains sufficient sources of protein, such as grain, legumes, and dairy.
The most important areas to consider when gaining lean muscle are:
1) Eating sufficient energy (calories)
a. The body needs energy to perform high-quality training. This will have to be increased so there is a surplus (more energy consumed than burnt ) in order to provide for the added requirements of building muscle.

135

b. Ensuring adequate carb intake is essential for bulking up – recover similarly as you would for a high-intensity session or a match to ensure adequate energy intake

2) Choose high-quality proteins
a. It is important that the proteins chosen provide all of the essential amino acids and have a high biological value. This is necessary for maximising protein synthesis.
b. Increases in protein synthesis are maximised by providing fast-release proteins after weights-training; over and above gains achieved by eating carbohydrate. Certain proteins, such as those in milk and whey protein, release their amino acids particularly fast...
Good sources include:
i. Dairy, meats, eggs, mixed vegetarian sources (e.g. beans + bread + cous- cous)
ii. Whey protein – Fast release protein, while convenience sports foods may help with frequent feeds

## 3) EAT PROTEIN WITHIN MINUTES OF TRAINING!
a. Optimal effects on protein metabolism have been seen from consuming protein within the first hour of recovery; after this time, protein synthesis will be greatly reduced!
b. Having a small intake of protein before weights training is also beneficial, although this needs to be low enough to prevent you feeling bloated and to allow sufficient intensity during training...

4) Frequency of feeding – eat OFTEN
a. Optimal protein requirements for muscle gain are relatively low - only 1.7g per Kilo. You would consume this if you consumed sufficient calories, even if you only ate bread (grains are actually quite high protein!).
b. Far more important is FREQUENCY OF EATING
As well as eating protein close to training sessions, consuming frequent protein servings over the day has been shown to be more beneficial for muscle metabolism than eating fewer, larger meals.
i. Try and schedule 4-6 meals per day when bulking up

## 136

## MUSCLE MEALS

The High-Carbohydrate + Protein meals given in the "recovery" section are perfect for bulking-up. Just increase the portions to ensure you are eating an excess of calories. As written above, another extremely important factor is eating protein frequently, and immediately after training. Rather than just meals then, snacking on quick convenient foods is vital!!

Easy To Eat, Convenient protein with carbs for after weights-training...

## SEAFOOD STIR-FRY
Serves 2-3:
• Grease the pan with the minimum sesame oil/coconut oil
• 2 types of shiitake mushrooms
• 1/2 red pepper, chopped
• 1 carrot, chopped
• 1 red onion, chopped
• 1/2 of each of a red and yellow pepper, shredded
• 60g beansprouts
• 1 clove of garlic
• 1 thumb of ginger
• 4 raw chilli
• 5 tsp chinese  ve-spice
• 1 tsp tamarind paste
• 100ml pineapple juice
• 1 tbsp  fish sauce
• 1 tsp peanut butter
• 1/2 can coconut water
• 300g mixed frozen seafood

How to cook:

Over a high heat, start cooking the garlic, chilli and ginger in a pan greased with the minimum coconut oil (as in the instructions). If you are planning on eating this without rice as part of a "low-carb day" then you can use extra sesame or coconut oil – the dish will benefit from the strong flavours.

Add all of the veg except the bean sprouts and stir fry over a very high heat – keep it moving so it doesn't stick!

Add the frozen seafood to the hot pan and stir it in. Add the coconut water, tamarind paste, Chinese 5 spice, fish sauce, peanut butter and pineapple juice. Simmer briefly to reduce the liquid then add and stir in the bean-sprouts. Finish with coriander. If you have trained hard (this is the ONLY time you should have simple sugars!), then you may want to add some ketchup or oyster sauce.

Depending on your activity that day, serve with a considered portion of mixed white & wild rice that's been boiled with some cardamom seeds. Alternatively, increase the portion of protein per serving, and add some cashew nuts for a higher fat, lower carb meal.

Vegetarians can replace the seafood with tofu/tempeh or even egg – stir in 1-2 beaten eggs per person into the stir-fry right at the end.

138

## SMOKED SALMON WITH RED-CABBAGE SALAD
Serves 3-4
- 200g Smoked Salmon
- 1/4 red cabbage, finely chopped
- 1 carrot, very thinly sliced
- 1 small handful walnuts
- 1 small handful raisins
- 1/2 bag baby spinach
- Dressing:
- 2 tbsp sesame oil
- 1 tbsp teriyaki marinade
- 2 tbsp balsamic vinegar
- 2 tsp soy sauce
1 dsp sundried tomatoes, chopped

How to cook:
Chop the salad ingredients, except the spinach leaves, and mix the dressing ingredients in a jar. You could even start chopping some of the veg for the stir-fry (below) to save time.
You can eat this on the same evening – in which case plate up with the cabbage, leaves and dressing. If preparing in advance, leave the cabbage and salmon mixture separate to the leaves and dressing – mix this immediately before consuming to stop sogginess! You could even use this as a filling for a wrap for the week's packed lunch.

For more nutritional advice and information visit Matt Lovell's websites or Twitter page.

# FOOTBALL
# EQUIPMENT

140

## ABOUT SPORTING EQUIPMENT

As with all sports you'll need the equipment to play them, and over the years sporting equipment has become a multi- billion pound business and with huge global brands cashing in and making all kinds of extra equipment, so it's often hard to see what is a necessity and what isn't, making you pay extra for something that you may never use.

So here is a list of equipment and what its does, so that you can make a more calculated decision on what your buying.

## FUNDAMENTAL FOOTBALL EQUIPMENT

• Ball
• Boots
• Shin pads
• Extras like goals, bibs, all the different type cones etc, are there to help if you can afford it, but there are ways in which you can use something else to help you instead.

## BALLS

There are many different sizes of footballs.
• Size 3 footballs are for children aged roughly between 4-7
• Size 4 footballs are for children aged roughly between 8-12
• Size 5 footballs are for teenagers 13 and upwards to mens/womens football.

One reason for all these sizes is to ease the amount of pressure you are taking on your joints, so young children between the age of 4-7 are not kicking a ball that weighs too much and is not too big in size for them, so they can develop their body and football skills.
There are different types of footballs: leather, rubber and indoor ones are the most common ones used.

Playing with an indoor football on concrete, will rip the outside of the ball apart very quickly and playing with a leather ball on gravel will also rip the outside very quickly so try and use the right ball for the right surface otherwise you'll end up ripping it apart and have to buy a new one.

Indoor footballs are exactly that, for indoors ie sports halls.
Rubber footballs are for outdoors concrete, gravel and hardwearing pitches.
Leather footballs are grass and Astroturf pitches

## BOOTS

There are many different types of boots made by many different sports brands Nike, Adidas, Puma and Reebok to name a few. With all these different companies making so many different types of boots it can be confusing to now what boots to buy your child so here is a quick breakdown.

When buying football boots its good for you take a pair of football socks with you so that you get a real feel for the size of the boots that you are going to purchase. Try and get the boot to fit with about a half and inch spare room at the front to allow for good blood circulation to the toes.( about a thumb nail size)
Check with the manager/coach of the team to find out what kind of surfaces you will be playing on before you go and buy your football boots because you can't play with certian boots on certain types of grounds. eg studs on astro turf.

143

## STUDDED BOOTS

Studded football boots or studs are for wearing on grass pitches, especially when the pitch is soft or wet, if worn on a dry pitch they can cause blisters amongst other things.
You can change the studs at the bottom and get longer or metal ones for better grip.

144

## MOULDED BOOTS

Moulded boots or moulds are for wearing on grass, hard grass, Astroturf, certain 4G and 3G football pitches. They're more of an all-round boot and a favourite for most players. They are a soft flexible boot and very comfortable, which is what makes them such a good boot to have. If they are worn on very wet/muddy ground they can become slippery.

## BLADES

Blades are a new style of boot, which is in-between a mould and studded boot; they are generally made of a plastic style bottom but can have metal tips. They are very light in weight and can be worn on grass and some Astros turf pitches mainly the new 4G ones. Some Astroturf pitches many not let you wear blades because they can rip the Astroturf.

## ASTROTURFS

Astroturfs or Astros are worn on Astroturf and 3G/4G surfaces. They generally have more grip then trainers, blades and moulded boots on Astroturf pitches. Astros can be worn on concrete pitches but can be slippery if the ground is a little wet, most gymnasiums and schools wont let you wear Astros as they leave marks on the floor so you can get a gum bottom version which won't mark the floor.

## TRAINERS

Flat trainers are for indoor gymnasiums and can be worn on Astroturf but will be slippery if the Astro is a bit wet. They are very comfortable and are the preferred footwear for freestylers and futsal players because they flexible and very soft. Can be worn in most schools gymnasiums and public gymnasiums because of the rubber bottoms.

## SHIN PADS

There are two types of shin-pad one with ankle protectors attached and one without ankles pads; which you can buy ankle protectors separately.

Generally shin-pads are made from plastic, the ankle protectors can be plastic or a
rubber. So its up to the individual preference on what kind of shin-pad they want to
wear, as it will be all about you own comfort.

The sizing on shin-pads is youth, boys, and men's and is written on the packaging
usually written in ages..

With shin-pads there are extras that you can buy, but these things are not a must
have.

Eg. Shin-pad tie-ups. What they do is hold your shin-pad up so you can play without
worrying that your shin-pad will fall down.

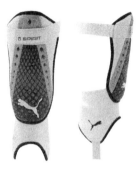

149

## A LITTLE ABOUT TRAINING EQUIPMENT

There are so many different types of training equipment all to help you with training different aspects of the body and training your skills. The costs are all different
depending on where you get them. Whether it's from the Internet or walking in to a
sports shop.
But I would say that these are the most important ones and the ones that you can
use in many different ways.

### CONES,
Cones are for marking out different exercises and marking out pitch sizes or marking out a football drills.

### POLES,
Poles are used for marking out pitches and goals but can also be used for running
exercisers as pretend opponents.

### LADDER,
The ladder is mainly used for speed training but it can also be used to help with
co-ordination.

150

# SUMMARY

151

A footballers life is one of excitement, fun, passion, bonding, friendship, winning, v.i.p treatment and all the luxuries in life that you would like. But it also has failure, disappointment, stress, abuse, pain, loneliness and things that can take your life in the wrong direction all of this at a young age.

But if you play football with the fun, love and passion that it was made for and have help from others in and around the game it can be made easier.

By following some of the guidelines set out in this book and the dream in your heart, you will have all the foundations and blueprints you need to be a happy and successful footballer. Enabling you to have the time of your life, enjoying and savouring every moment you have when you step out onto the pitch, training ground or any football environment.


Life is football and football is life to you, the things that your dreams are made of that money can't buy. These things you can achieve and make others aspire to. This is the biggest goal and one that will stay with you forever.


Good luck in whatever you do and wherever you become a professional or not. The footballing world is a big one and can take you all over the world  the most important thing is to love the game and enjoy what you do..

# EXTRA ADVICE

Throughout this book you have been given advice on many things that can happen on your journey. If you want to get extra advice on some of the subjects you have just read or there is other advice you seek you can look at my YouTube channel Dean Holness.

Also another place to have a looking is the FA and PFA websites, as they will also have links to other websites that will be able to answer many questions you may have.

# THANKS TO

Thank you to all of those that helped me to become a professional footballer and have a career after football enabling me to write this book.

Andy Ansah, Peter Smith, Aaron Maines, Matt Lovell, Brian Walpole, Danny Mills, Martin Keown, Paul Davis, Matthew Buck, George Bowyer, Terry Angus, Chris Joslin, Daniel Webb, Leon Jiber, Nathlie Heseltine, Gary Dixon, Harry Redknapp, Teddy Sheringham, Hayden Mullins, Clinton Morrison, Leon Mckenzie, Daniel Wood, Jamie Cureton, James Evans, Richard Philpys, Carl Leaburn, Chris Kamara, Mark Hall, Charlie MacDonald, Lara Gosling, Anthony Mac, Laura Marie Linck, Ben Coppin, Eleanor Wanless, Rebecca Sparkes, Jenna Hussey, Natalie Collins, Greg Regan, Marc Bircham, Carl Leaburn, Hussein Isa, Sagi Burton, Liz Holness, Eddie McClemments, Puma, SportsOnScreen Team, Sky O2 Team, Wasserman, New Era & The PFA

To my beautiful family without you i'd be nothing, thank you for you patience
and support over so many years.
love you X

155

illustration by Ben Coppin
Instagram: @benksycartoons
Email: benksycartoons@gmail.com